25 Jobs That Have It All

Ferguson Publishing Company
Chicago, Illinois

Managing Editor-Career Publications: Andrew Morkes
Cover Design: Sam Concialdi
Interior Design: Carol Yehling
Indexer: Sandi Schroeder
Proofreader: Bonnie Needham

Copyright © 2001 Ferguson Publishing Company

Library of Congress Cataloging-in-Publication Data
25 jobs that have it all
    p. cm.
  Includes index.
  ISBN 0-89434-327-0
   1. Vocational guidance. 2. Occupations--Forecasting. 3. Employment forecast-
ing. [1. Vocational guidance.] I. Title: Twenty five jobs that have it all. II.
Ferguson Publishing Company.

HF5382 .A15 2000
331.7'02--dc21   00-039387

Printed in the United States of America

Published and distributed by:
Ferguson Publishing Company
200 West Jackson, 7th Floor
Chicago, Illinois 60606
800-306-9941
http://www.fergpubco.com

X-9

Table of Contents

Introduction 1

Advertising Account Executives 3

College Professors 8

Commodities Brokers 15

Computer Network Administrators 24

Computer Programmers 32

Computer Systems/Programmer Analysts 39

Database Specialists 47

Electrical and Electronics Engineers 53

Financial Services Brokers 63

Graphic Designers 68

Hardware Engineers 75

Health Care Managers 80

Illustrators 86

Management Analysts and Consultants 93

Paralegals 100

Physicians 107

Police Officers 117

Registered Nurses 126

Secondary School Teachers 134

Social Workers 141

Software Designers 150

Software Engineers 157

Special Education Teachers 165

Technical Support Specialists 172

Writers and Editors 180

Index 191

Introduction

What is your idea of a job that has it all? If you answered high pay, fast growth, and the most new jobs, you're on the right track. With the help of U.S. Department of Labor statistics, we have assembled a group of careers that offer this unique combination. *25 Jobs That Have It All* covers careers in all of the top industries, from computers and health care to education and design to business and social services.

What do we mean by high pay, fast growth, and most new jobs?

High pay. When you choose a career, compensation is always an important consideration. The careers in *25 Jobs That Have It All* offer higher salaries than the national average of $29,900 a year in 2000. A good example of a high-paying job profiled in this book is Physicians, who earn a median income of over $164,000 a year.

Fast growth. Fast growing occupations, according to the Department of Labor, "usually have better employment prospects and conditions more favorable for mobility and advancement." The careers in *25 Jobs That Have It All* will grow faster than the average (an increase of 21 to 35 percent) or much faster than the average (an increase of 36 percent or more) through 2008, according to the Department of Labor. The average growth rate for all occupations is 12 percent. Computer Systems/Programmer Analyst is an excellent example of a career with fast growth that is included in this book. The Department of Labor predicts that this career will grow by a whopping 99 percent through 2008.

Most new jobs. Many careers are fast growing but do not offer a large number of openings to new job applicants. The career of Desktop Publishing Specialist is a good example. Although faster than average growth is predicted for this career, there will only be 19,000 new positions available to new workers—making your job search a real challenge.

The careers in *25 Jobs That Have It All* are not only fast growing, but also offer good employment prospects due to the large number of new positions available to prospective workers. These job openings result from both employment growth and replacement needs (workers who retire, transfer to other occupations, or return to school). A career in the most new jobs category included in *25 Jobs That Have It All* is Technical Support Specialists. The Department of Labor predicts that over 439,000 new positions will be available in this career by 2008.

The following paragraphs describe the major headings used throughout *25 Jobs That Have It All*. These headings will help you find the information you want quickly and easily.

The **Overview** section is a brief introductory description of the duties and responsibilities of someone in this career. Oftentimes, a career may have a variety of job titles. When that is the case, alternate career titles are presented in this section.

The Job section describes primary and secondary duties of the job, the types of tools, machinery, or equipment used to perform this job, and other types of workers in this environment. Growing subfields or subspecialties of this career are also described.

The **Requirements** section details the formal educational requirements—from high school diploma to advanced college degree—that are necessary for you to become employed in this field. This section provides information on how you can receive training if a college degree is not required, via on-the-job training, apprenticeships, the armed forces, or other activities. Certification, licensing, and continuing education requirements are also covered. Finally, the Requirements section recommends personal qualities that will give you an extra advantage in this field.

In the **Exploring** section, you will find a variety of ways, such as periodicals, summer jobs and programs, volunteer opportunities, associations, and clubs and hobbies, to explore the field further before you invest time and money in education and training.

The **Employers** section lists major employers of workers in the field.

The **Starting Out** section offers tips on how to land your first job, be it through newspaper ads, the Internet, college placement offices, or through personal contacts. This section explains how the average person finds employment in this field.

The **Advancement** section describes possible career paths and the experience you will need—advanced training or outside education—to move up in this field.

The **Earnings** section lists salary ranges for beginning, mid-range, and experienced workers in this field. Fringe benefits, such as paid vacation and sick days, health insurance, pensions, and profit sharing plans, are covered.

In the **Work Environment** section you will see what a typical day on the job is like. Is indoor or outdoor work required? Are safety measures and equipment such as protective clothing necessary? Is the job in a quiet office or on a noisy assembly line? What are the standard hours of work? Are overtime and weekend work often required? Is travel frequent? If so, to where, and for how long?

The **Outlook** section predicts the potential long-term employment outlook for the field. Job growth terms follow those used in the *Occupational Outlook Handbook*.

In the last section, **For More Information,** you'll find the names, street addresses, phone numbers, email, and Web addresses of a variety of associations, government agencies, or unions that can provide further information regarding educational requirements, accreditation and certification, and other general information about the career you've just read about.

We hope that *25 Jobs That Have It All* will increase your knowledge of careers and help you to make informed choices regarding your future. Remember that the world of work is always changing. This book is only the beginning of your career education. To stay informed, you will need to gather information from the associations listed at the end of each article, talk with workers in these fields, and continue to research these careers and others via the Internet or your school or local library. Only the educated worker will stay ahead in today's—and tomorrow's—job market.

Good luck in your career exploration!

The Editors

Advertising Account Executives

Overview

The advertising account executive *coordinates and over-sees everything related to a client's advertising account and acts as the primary liaison between the agency and the client. Account executives are also responsible for building and maintaining professional relationships among clients and coworkers to ensure the successful completion of major ad campaigns and the assurance of continued business with clients.*

The Job

Account executives track the day-to-day progress of the overall advertising campaigns of their clients. Together with a staff commonly consisting of a creative director, an art director, a copywriter, researchers, and production specialists, the account executive monitors all client accounts from beginning to end.

Before an advertising campaign is actually launched, a lot of preparatory work is needed. Account executives must familiarize themselves with their clients' products and services, target markets, goals, competitors, and preferred media. Together with the agency team, the account executive gathers this information by conducting research and holding initial meetings with clients. Once all the needed information has been gathered, the team, coordinated by the account executive, analyzes the market potential and presents recommendations to the client.

After an advertising strategy has been determined and all terms have been agreed upon, the agency's creative staff goes to work, developing ideas and producing various ads to present to the client. During this time, the account executive is working with media buyers in order to develop a schedule for the project and make sure that the costs involved are within the client's budget.

When the ad campaign has been approved by the client, production can begin. In addition to supervising and coordinating the work of copywriters, editors, graphic artists, production specialists, and other employ-ees on the agency team, the account executive must also write reports and draft business correspondence, follow up on all client meetings, interact with outside vendors, and ensure that all pieces of the advertising cam-paign clearly communicate the desired message. In sum, the account exec-utive is responsible for making sure that the client is satisfied. This may require making modifications to the campaign, revising cost estimates and events schedules, and redirecting the efforts of the creative staff.

In addition to their daily responsibilities of tracking and handling clients' advertising campaigns, account executives must also develop and bring in new business, keep up-to-date on current advertising trends, eval-uate the effectiveness of advertising programs, and track sales figures.

Requirements

High School

You can prepare for a career as an advertising account executive by taking a variety of courses at the high school level. General liberal arts courses, such as English, journalism, communication, economics, psychology, busi-ness, social science, and mathematics, are important for aspiring advertis-ing account executives.

Postsecondary Training

Most advertising agencies hire college graduates whose degrees can vary widely, from English, journalism, or marketing to business administration, speech, or fine arts. Courses in psychology, sociology, economics, and any art medium are also helpful. Some positions require a graduate degree in advertising, art, or marketing. Others may call for experience in a particu-lar field, such as health care, insurance, or retail.

While most employers prefer a broad liberal arts background with courses in marketing, market research, sales, consumer behavior, commu-nication, and technology, many also seek employees who already have some work experience. Those candidates who have completed on-the-job internships at agencies or have developed portfolios will have a competi-tive edge.

Other Requirements

While account executives do not need to have the same degree of artistic skill or knowledge as art directors or graphic designers, they must be imag-inative and understand the communication of art and photography in order to direct the overall progress of an ad campaign. They should also be able to work under pressure, motivate employees, solve problems, and demonstrate flexibility, good judgment, decisiveness, and patience.

Account executives must be aware of trends and be interested in the business climate and the psychology of making purchases. In addition, they should be able to write clearly, make effective presentations, and communicate persuasively. It is also helpful to stay abreast of the various computer programs used in advertising design and management.

Exploring

For those aspiring to jobs in the advertising industry, some insight can be gained by taking writing and art courses offered either in school or by private organizations. In addition to the theoretical ideas and techniques that such classes can provide, you can actually apply what you learn by working full- or part-time at local department stores or newspaper offices.

Employers

Advertising agencies all across the country and abroad employ advertising account executives. Of the 22,000 agencies in the United States, the large firms located in New York, Chicago, and Los Angeles tend to dominate the advertising industry. However, four out of five organizations each employ fewer than ten people. These "small shops" offer employment opportunities for account executives with experience, talent, and flexibility.

Starting Out

Many people aspiring to the job of account executive participate in internships or begin as assistant executives, allowing them to work with clients, study the market, and follow up on client service. This work gives students a good sense of the rhythm of the job and the type of work required of account executives.

College graduates, with or without experience, can start their job search in the school placement office. Staff there can set up interviews and help polish resumes.

The advertising arena is rich with opportunities. When looking for employment, you don't have to target agencies; instead, many large companies employ advertising staff. If you want to work at an agency, you'll find the competition intense for jobs there. Once hired, however, account executives often participate in special training programs that both initiate them and help them to succeed.

Advancement

Since practical experience and a broad base of knowledge are often required of advertising account executives, many employees work their way up through the company, from assistant to account executive to account manager and finally to department head. In smaller agencies, where promotions depend on experience and leadership, advancement may occur slowly. In larger firms, management training programs are often required for advancement. Continuing education is occasionally offered to account executives in these firms, often through local colleges or special seminars provided by professional societies.

Earnings

An assistant account executive earns between $20,000 to $25,000 annually, while an experienced employee can expect to earn about $54,300, according to the *Occupational Outlook Handbook.* In smaller agencies, the salary may be much lower (in the mid-twenties), and in larger firms, it is often much higher (sometimes over $100,000). Salaries also vary by region, with account executives in the north central part of the United States making an average of $33,800 at the low end and those in the West earning an average of $45,500 at the high end. Salary bonuses are common for account executives. Benefits typically include vacation and sick leave, health and life insurance, and a retirement plan.

Work Environment

It is not uncommon for advertising account executives to work long hours, including evenings and weekends. Informal meetings with clients, for example, frequently take place after normal business hours. In addition, some travel may be required when clients are based in other cities or states or when account executives must attend industry conferences.

Advertising agencies are usually highly charged with energy and are both physically and psychologically exciting places to work. The account executive must work with others as a team in a creative environment where a lot of ideas are exchanged among fellow employees.

As deadlines are critical in advertising, it is important that account executives possess the ability to handle pressure and stress effectively. Patience and flexibility are also essential, as are organization and time management skills.

Outlook

The growth of the advertising industry depends on the health of the economy. In a thriving economy, advertising funds are available, consumers tend to respond to advertising campaigns, and new products and services that require promotion are increasingly developed. With the U.S. economy continuing to thrive, employment in the advertising industry is expected to increase at a rate that is faster than the average for all occupations through the year 2008.

Most opportunities for advertising account executives will be in larger cities, such as Chicago, New York, and Los Angeles, that enjoy a high concentration of business. Competition for these jobs, however, will be intense. The successful candidate will be a college graduate with a lot of creativity, strong communications skills, and extensive experience in the advertising industry. Those able to speak another language will have an edge because of the increasing supply of products and services offered in foreign markets.

For More Information

The AAF is the professional advertising association that binds the mutual interests of corporate advertisers, agencies, media companies, suppliers, and academia. Visit their Web site to learn more about internships, scholarships, and awards.

American Advertising Federation (AAF)
1101 Vermont Avenue, NW, Suite 500
Washington, DC 20005-6306
Tel: 202-898-0089
Web: http://www.aaf.org

The AAAA is the management-oriented national trade organization representing the advertising agency business.

American Association of Advertising Agencies (AAAA)
405 Lexington Avenue, 18th Floor
New York, NY 10174-1801
Tel: 212-682-2500
Web: http://www.aaaa.org/

The AMA is an international professional society of individual members with an interest in the practice, study, and teaching of marketing.

American Marketing Association (AMA)
311 South Wacker Drive, Suite 5800
Chicago, IL 60606
Web: http://www.ama.org

College Professors

College professors *instruct undergraduate and graduate students in specific subjects at colleges and universities. They are responsible for lecturing classes, leading small seminar groups, and creating and grading examinations. They also may carry on research, write for publication, and aid in administration.*

The Job

College and university faculty members teach at junior colleges or at four-year colleges and universities. At four-year institutions, most faculty members are *assistant professors, associate professors,* or *full professors.* These three types of professorships differ in regards to status, job responsibilities, and salary. Assistant professors are new faculty members who are working to get tenure (status as a permanent professor); they seek to advance to associate then full professorships.

College professors perform three main functions: teaching, advising, and research. Their most important responsibility is to teach students. Their role within a college department will determine the level of courses they teach and the number of courses per semester. Most professors work with students at all levels, from college freshmen to graduate students. They may head several classes a semester, or only a few a year. Some of their classes will have large enrollment, while graduate seminars may only consist of 12 or fewer students. Though college professors may spend fewer than 10 hours a week in the actual classroom, they spend many hours preparing lectures and lesson plans, grading papers and exams, and preparing grade reports. They also schedule office hours during the week to be available to students outside of the lecture hall, and they meet with students individually throughout the semester. In the classroom, professors lecture, lead discussions, administer exams, and assign textbook reading and other research. In some courses, they rely heavily on laboratories to transmit course material.

Another important responsibility is advising students. Not all faculty members serve as advisers, but those who do must set aside large blocks of time to guide students through the program. College professors that serve as advisers may have any number of students assigned to them, from fewer than 10 to more than 100, depending on the administrative policies of the college. Their responsibility may involve looking over a planned program of studies to make sure the students meet requirements for graduation, or it may involve working intensively with each student on many aspects of college life.

The third responsibility of college and university faculty members is research and publication. Faculty members who are heavily involved in research programs sometimes are assigned a smaller teaching load. College professors publish their research findings in various scholarly journals. They also write books based on their research or on their own knowledge and experience in the field. Most textbooks are written by college and university teachers. In arts-based programs, such as master's of fine arts programs in painting, writing, and theater, professors practice their craft and exhibit their art work in various ways. For example, a painter or photographer will have gallery showings, while a poet will publish in literary journals.

Publishing a significant amount of work has been the traditional standard by which assistant professors prove themselves worthy of becoming permanent, tenured faculty, and so typically, pressure to publish is greatest for assistant professors. Pressure to publish increases again if an associate professor wishes to be considered for a promotion to full professorship.

In recent years, some liberal arts colleges have recognized that the pressure to publish is taking faculty away from their primary duties to the students, and these institutions have begun to place a decreasing emphasis on publishing and more on performance in the classroom. Professors in junior colleges face less pressure to publish than those in four-year institutions.

Some faculty members eventually rise to the position of department chair, where they govern the affairs of an entire department, such as English, mathematics, or biological sciences. Department chairs, faculty, and other professional staff members are aided in their myriad duties by graduate assistants, who may help develop teaching materials, conduct research, give examinations, teach lower-level courses, and carry out other activities.

Some college professors may also conduct classes in an extension program. In such a program, they teach evening and weekend courses for the benefit of people who otherwise would not be able to take advantage of the institution's resources. They may travel away from the campus and meet with a group of students at another location. They may work full time for the extension division, or may divide the time between on-campus and off-campus teaching.

An extension work instructor teaches through correspondence. Correspondence courses usually are available only to undergraduate students. In a standard course of study for the subject, a college professor's responsibility would be to grade the papers that the student sends in at periodic intervals and to advise the student of progress. Extension work instructors may perform this service in addition to other duties or may be assigned to correspondence work as a major teaching responsibility.

The instructor in a junior college has many of the same kinds of responsibilities as does the teacher in a four-year college or university. Because junior colleges offer only a two-year program, they only teach undergraduates.

Requirements

High School

Your high school's college-preparatory program likely includes courses in English, science, foreign language, math, and government. In addition, you should take courses in speech to get a sense of what it will be like to lecture to a group of students. Your school's debate team can also help you develop public speaking skills, along with research skills.

Postsecondary Training

At least one advanced degree in your field of study is required to be a professor in a college or university. The master's degree is considered the minimum standard, and graduate work beyond the master's is usually desirable. A doctorate is required to advance in academic rank above instructor in most institutions.

In the last year of your undergraduate program, you'll apply to graduate programs in your area of study. Standards for admission to a graduate program can be high, and the competition heavy, depending on the school. Once accepted into a program, your responsibilities will be similar to those of your professors—in addition to attending seminars, you'll research, prepare articles for publication, and teach some undergraduate courses.

The faculty member in a junior college may be employed with only a master's degree. Advancement in responsibility and in salary, however, is more likely to come to those who have earned a doctorate.

Other Requirements

You should enjoy reading, writing, and researching—not only will you spend many years studying in school, but your whole career will be based on communicating your thoughts and ideas. People skills are important because you'll be dealing directly with students, administrators, and other faculty members on a daily basis. You should feel comfortable in a role of authority, and possess self-confidence.

Exploring

Your high school teachers use many of the same skills as college professors, so talk to your teachers about their careers and their college experiences. You can develop your own teaching experience by volunteering with a community center, working at a daycare center, or working at a summer camp. Also, spend some time on a college campus to get a sense of the environment. Write to colleges for their admissions brochures and course catalogs; read about the faculty members and the courses they teach. Before visiting college campuses, make arrangements to speak to professors who teach courses that interest you. These professors may allow you to sit in on their classes and observe. Also, make appointments with college advisers, and with people in the admissions and recruitment offices.

Employers

Employment opportunities vary based on area of study and education. Most universities have many different departments that hire faculty. With a doctorate, a number of publications, and a record of good teaching, professors should find opportunities in universities all across the country—there are more than 3,800 colleges and universities in the United States. Professors teach in undergraduate and graduate programs. The teaching jobs at doctoral institutions are usually better paying and more prestigious. The most sought-after positions are those that offer tenure. Teachers that only have a master's degree will be limited to opportunities with junior colleges, community colleges, and some small private institutions.

Starting Out

While in graduate school, you'll be working toward developing your curriculum vitae (a detailed, academic resume). You'll write and publish, assist with research, attend conferences, and gain teaching experience and recommendations. While finishing your graduate program, you'll apply for teaching positions. For most positions at four-year institutions, you'll have to travel to large conferences where you'll be interviewed by several professors from the universities to which you have applied.

Because of the competition for tenure-track positions, you may have to work for a few years in temporary positions, visiting various schools as an adjunct professor. Some professional associations maintain lists of teaching opportunities in their areas. They may also make lists of applicants available to college administrators looking to fill an available position.

Advancement

The normal pattern of advancement is from instructor to assistant professor, to associate professor, to full professor. All four academic ranks are concerned primarily with teaching and research. College faculty members who have an interest in and a talent for administration may be advanced to chair of a department, or to dean of their college. A few become college or university presidents or other types of administrators.

The instructor is usually an inexperienced college teacher. He or she may hold a doctorate or may have completed all the Ph.D. requirements except for the dissertation. Most colleges look upon the rank of instructor as the period during which the college is trying the teacher out. Instructors usually are advanced to the position of assistant professors within three to four years. Assistant professors are given up to about six years to prove themselves worthy of tenure, and if they do so, they become associate professors. Some professors choose to remain at the associate level. Others strive to become full professors and receive greater status, salary, and responsibilities.

Most colleges have clearly defined promotion policies from rank to rank for faculty members and many have written statements about the number of years in which instructors and assistant professors may remain in grade. Administrators in many colleges hope to encourage younger faculty members to increase their skills and competencies and thus to qualify for the more responsible positions of associate professor and full professor.

Earnings

Both the *Chronicle of Higher Education* and the American Association of University Professors (AAUP) conduct annual surveys of the salaries of college professors. With the 1998 survey, the *Chronicle* found that full professors at public universities received an average of $69,924 a year, while professors at private universities received $84,970 a year. Associate professors received an average of $50,186 annually at public universities, and

$56,517 at private. For assistant professors, the average salaries were $42,335 public, $47,387 private.

The AAUP's 1999 survey found that salary levels had increased from the previous year, but remain 4.4 percent lower than 25 years ago, when figures are adjusted for inflation. And professors earn 42 percent less than those in comparable professions. The AAUP survey found that professors in doctoral institutions made an average of $66,991 a year, compared to $53,454 for those in master's institutions, and $48,257 for those in undergraduate institutions. Professors working in the Western Pacific states, such as California and Oregon, earned the most, followed by those working in New England. The survey found the average pay to be the lowest in such Southern states as Alabama, Kentucky, and Mississippi.

Work Environment

A college or university is usually a pleasant place in which to work. Campuses bustle with all types of activities and events, stimulating ideas, and a young, energetic population. Much prestige comes with success as a professor and scholar; professors have the respect of students, colleagues, and others in their community.

Depending on the size of the department, college professors may have their own office, or they may have to share an office with one or more colleagues. Their department may provide them with a computer, Internet access, and research assistants. College professors are also able to do much of their office work at home. They can arrange their schedule around class hours, academic meetings, and the established office hours when they meet with students. Most college teachers work more than 40 hours each week. Although college professors may only teach two or three classes a semester, they spend many hours preparing for lectures, examining student work, and conducting research.

Outlook

The U.S. Department of Labor predicts faster than average growth for college and university professors through the year 2008. College enrollment is projected to rise from 14.6 million in 1998 to 16.1 million in 2008—an increase of about 10 percent. Competition for jobs—especially full-time, tenure-track positions at 4-year universities—will be very strong. Additionally, opportunities for college teachers will be good in areas—such as engineering, business, computer science, and health science—that offer strong career prospects in the world of work.

A number of factors threaten to change the way colleges and universities hire faculty. Some university leaders are developing more business-based methods of running their schools, focusing on profits and budgets. This can affect college professors in a number of ways. One of the biggest effects is in the replacement of tenure-track faculty positions with part-time instructors. These part-time instructors include adjunct faculty, visiting professors, and graduate students. Organizations such as AAUP and the American Federation of Teachers (AFT), are working to prevent the loss of these full-time jobs, as well as to help part-time instructors receive better pay and benefits. Other issues involve the development of long-distance education departments in many schools. Though these correspondence courses have become very popular in recent years, many professionals believe that students in distance education programs receive only a second-rate education. A related concern is about the proliferation of computers in the classroom. Some courses consist only of instruction by computer software and the Internet. The effects of these alternative methods on the teaching profession will be offset somewhat by the expected increases in college enrollment in coming years.

For More Information

To read about the issues affecting college professors, visit the Web sites of these organizations:

American Association of University Professors
1012 14th Street, NW, Suite 500
Washington, DC 20005-3465
Tel: 202-737-5900
Email: aaup@aaup.org
Web: http://www.aaup.org

American Federation of Teachers
555 New Jersey Avenue, NW
Washington, DC 20001
Tel: 202-879-4400
Web: http://www.aft.org

Commodities Brokers

Commodities brokers, *also known as* futures commission merchants, *act as agents in carrying out purchases and sales of commodities for customers or traders. Commodities are primary goods that are either raw or partially refined. Such goods are produced by farmers, such as corn, wheat, or cattle, or mined from the earth, such as gold, copper, or silver. Brokers, who may work at a brokerage house, on the floor of a commodities exchange, or independently, are paid a fee or commission for acting as the middleman to conduct and complete the trade.*

The Job

A futures contract is an agreement to deliver a particular commodity, such as wheat, pork bellies, or coffee, at a specific date, time, and place. For example, a farmer might sell his oats before they are sowed (known as hedging) because he can't predict what kind of price he'll be able to demand later on. If the weather is favorable and crops are good, he'll have competition, which will drive prices down. If there is a flood or drought, oats will be scarce, driving the price up. He wants to ensure fair price for his product to protect his business and limit his risk since he can't predict what will happen.

On the other side of the equation is the user of the oats, perhaps a cereal manufacturer, who purchases these contracts for a delivery of oats at some future date. The third party is the speculator, or *trader,* who is neither a producer or consumer. Traders enter the market to make a profit by anticipating the direction of the commodity's price. Producers and consumers do not correspond to a one-to-one ratio, and it is the trader who acts as the middleman in the buying and selling of contracts.

Brokers place the trades of speculators who cannot place their own if they are not a member of an exchange. Brokers are paid a fee or commission for acting as the agent in making the sale. There are two broad categories of brokers, though they are becoming less distinct. *Full service bro-*

kers provide considerable research to clients, offer price quotes, give trading advice, and assist the customer in making trading decisions. *Discount brokers* simply fill the orders as directed by clients. Some brokers offer intermediate levels of optional services on a sliding scale of commission, such as market research and strategic advice.

In general, brokers are responsible for taking and carrying out all commodity orders and being available on call to do so; reporting back to the client upon fulfilling the order request; keeping the client abreast of breaking news; maintaining account balances and other financial data; and obtaining market information when needed and informing the client about important changes in the marketplace.

Brokers can work on the floor of a commodity futures exchange—the marketplace where contracts are bought and sold—for a brokerage house, or independently. The exchange houses the trading floor where brokers transact their business in the trading pit. There are 11 domestic exchanges, with the main ones in Chicago, Kansas City, New York, and Minneapolis. A broker or trader must be a member of an exchange, which is a private membership organization. Membership is limited to a specific and small number of individuals who must purchase or rent a seat on the floor, which is quite expensive. Purchasing a seat on the Chicago Exchange, for example, costs $760,000 and also entails a thorough investigation of the applicant's credit standing, financial background, and character. Most brokers, therefore, work for a brokerage house dealing in futures. These may be companies like Merrill Lynch or Dean Witter, which deal in stocks, bonds, commodities, and other investments, or smaller houses such as R.J. O'Brien, which handle only commodities.

Companies can also have a seat on the exchange, and they have their own *floor brokers* in the pit to carry out trades for the brokerage house. Brokers in the company take orders from the public for buying or selling a contract and promptly pass it on to the floor broker in the pit of the exchange. Brokers also have the choice of running their own business. Known as *introducing brokers,* they handle their own clients and trades and use brokerage houses to place their orders. Introducing brokers earn a fee by soliciting business trades, but they don't directly handle the customer's funds.

Requirements

High School

Although there are no formal educational requirments for becoming a broker, a high school and a college degree are strongly recommended.

Commodities brokers need to have a wide range of knowledge, covering such areas as economics, world politics, and sometimes even the weather. To begin to develop this broad-base of knowledge, start in high school by taking history, math, science, and business classes. Since commodities brokers are constantly working with people to make a sale, take English classes to enhance your communication skills. In addition to this course work, you might also consider getting a part-time job working in a sales position. Such a job will also give you the chance to hone your communication and sales skills.

Postsecondary Training

The vast majority of brokers have a college degree. While there is no "commodities broker major," you can improve your chances of obtaining a job in this field by studying economics, finance, or business administration while in college. Keep in mind that you should continue to develop your understanding of politics and technologies, so government and computer classes will also be useful.

Brokerage firms look for employees who have sales ability, strong communication skills, and self-confidence. Commodities is often a second career for many people who have demonstrated these qualities in other positions.

Certification or Licensing

To become a commodities broker, it is necessary to pass the National Commodities Futures Examination (the Series 3 exam) to become eligible to satisfy the registration requirements of federal, state, and industry regulatory agencies. The test covers market and trading knowledge, as well as rules and regulations. The test costs $75 and is available through the National Futures Association (NFA). The Commodity Education Institute offers week-long courses to prepare for the exam. Brokers must also register with the National Futures Association. Floor brokers, however, are not required to take the exam and are instead put through a rigorous training program at the exchange.

Other Requirements

Brokers must possess a combination of research and money management skills. They need to be attentive to detail and have a knack for analyzing data. Strong communications and sales skills are important as well, as brokers make money by convincing people to let them place their trades. An interest in and awareness of the world around them is also a contributing factor to a broker's success, as commodities are influenced by everything from political decisions and international news to social trends and weather.

Brokers must also be emotionally stable to work in such a volatile environment. They need to be persistent, aggressive, and comfortable taking risks and dealing with failure. Strong, consistent, and independent judgment is also key. Brokers must be disciplined hard workers, able to comb through reams of market reports and charts to gain a thorough understanding of their particular commodity and the mechanics of the marketplace. They also need to be outspoken and assertive, able to yell out prices loudly and energetically on the trading floor and command attention.

Exploring

Students interested in commodities trading should visit one of the futures exchanges. All of them offer public tours, and you'll get to see up close just how the markets work and the roles of the players involved. All the exchanges offer educational programs and publications, and most have a page on the World Wide Web (See "For More Information"). The Chicago Mercantile Exchange publishes *The Merc at Work,* the full text of which is also available on the Internet, as well as many other educational handbooks and pamphlets. There are hundreds of industry newsletters and magazines available (such as *Futures Magazine*), and many offer free samples of publications or products. Read what trading advisors have to say and how they say it. Learn their lingo and gain an understanding of the marketplace. If you have any contacts in the industry, arrange to spend a day with a broker. Watch him or her work, and you'll learn how orders are entered, processed, and reported.

Do your own research. Adopt a commodity, chart its prices, test some of your own ideas, and analyze the marketplace. There are also a variety of inexpensive software programs, as well as sites on the Web, that simulate trading.

Finally, consider a job as a *runner* during the summer before your freshman year in college. Runners transport the order, or "paper" from the phone clerk to the broker in the pit and relay information to and from members on the floor. This is the single best way to get hands-on experience in the industry.

Employers

Commodities brokers work on the floor of a commodity futures exchange, for brokerage houses, or independently.

Starting Out

College graduates can start working with a brokerage house as an associate and begin handling stocks. After several years they can take the certification exam and move into futures. Another option is to start as support staff, either at the exchange or the brokerage house. Sales personnel try to get customers to open accounts, and account executives develop and service customers for the brokerage firm. At the exchange, phone clerks receive incoming orders and communicate the information to the runners. Working in the back as an accountant, money manager, or member of the research staff is also another route. School placement offices may be able to assist graduates in finding jobs with brokerage houses. Applications may also be made directly to brokerage houses themselves.

Many successful brokers and traders began their careers as a runner, and each exchange has its own training program. Though the pay is low, runners learn the business very quickly with a hands-on experience not available in an academic classroom. Contact one of the commodities exchanges for information on becoming a runner.

Advancement

A broker who simply executes trades can advance to become a full-service broker. Through research and analysis and the accumulation of experience and knowledge about the industry, a broker can advance from an order filler and become a commodity trading advisor. A broker can also become a money manager and make all trading decisions for clients.

Within the exchange, a broker can become a *floor manager*, overseeing the processes of order-taking and information exchange. To make more money, a broker can also begin to place his or her own trades for his or her own private account, though the broker's first responsibility is to the customers.

Earnings

This is an entrepreneurial business. A broker's commission is based on the number of clients he or she recruits, the more they invest, and the amount of money they make. The sky's the limit. In recent years the most successful broker made $25 million. A typical salary for a newly hired employee in a brokerage might average $1,500 per month plus a 30 percent commission on sales. Smaller firms are likely to pay a smaller commission. The U.S. Department of Labor reports that the median annual earnings for securities, commodities, and financial services sales representatives were

$48,090 in 1998. The lowest 10 percent earned less than $22,600; the highest 10 percent earned more than $124,800 annually.

Working with the Chicago Board of Trade, the world's leading futures exchange, offers numerous benefits. Employees are eligible for vacation six months after employment and receive three weeks after three years. Employees are also paid for sick days, personal days, and eight holidays. During the summer months various departments offer flex time, allowing employees to take Fridays off by working longer hours during the week. Employees also receive numerous forms of insurance, including medical, life, and disability. Full tuition reimbursement is available as is a company-matched savings plan, a tax-deferred savings plan, and a pension program. Other large exchanges and brokerage houses offer similar combinations of benefits.

Work Environment

The trading floor is noisy and chaotic, as trading is done using an "open outcry" system. Every broker must be an auctioneer, yelling out his own price bids for purchases and sales. The highest bid wins and silences all the others. When a broker's primal scream is not heard, bids and offers can also be communicated with hand signals.

Brokers stand for most of the day, often in the same place, so that traders interested in their commodity can locate them easily. Each broker wears a distinctly colored jacket with a prominent identification badge. The letter on the badge identifies the broker and appears on the paperwork relating to the trade. Members of the exchange and employees of member firms wear red jackets. Some brokers and traders also have uniquely patterned jackets to further increase their visibility in the pit.

Brokers and traders do not have a nine-to-five job. While commodities trading on the exchange generally takes place from 9:00 AM to 1:00 PM, international trading runs from 2:45 PM to 6:50 AM.

In the rough and tumble world of the futures exchange, emotions run high as people often win or lose six-figure amounts within hours. Tension is fierce, the pace is frantic, and angry, verbal, and sometimes physical exchanges are not uncommon.

Outlook

The U.S. Bureau of Labor Statistics predicts much faster than the average growth—about 41 percent—for securities and financial sales representatives through the year 2008. Two major trends are affecting the future of the commodities industry: international growth and new technology.

Though the industry on the whole is small (50,000 firms as compared to the 400,000 firms in securities) and firms are sizing down, the number of exchanges has doubled in the last 10 years, and in 1998 there were 68 exchanges in 28 countries. The United States used to control 90 percent of the world's business, and now accounts for just 45 percent. Opportunities to manage commodities are no longer limited to the United States.

New commodities are also bursting onto the scene. During the 1980s, 186 new futures contracts were introduced. And nearly half of the total volume of trades were a product of these new contracts. Look for new types of commodities to continue to grow along with the move toward globalization, and for brokers to become highly specialized.

New computer and information technology is rapidly influencing and advancing the industry. A growing number of exchanges now use electronic systems to automate trades, and many use them exclusively. Many systems have unique features designed specifically to meet customers' needs. New technology, such as electronic order entry, hookups to overseas exchanges, and night trading, is rapidly evolving, offering brokers new ways to manage risk and provide price information.

For More Information

The Center provides information on workshops, home study courses, educational materials, and publications for futures and securities professionals. How to Become a Futures Broker *is an informative 24-page booklet (cost: $3) that discusses the National Commodity Futures Exam, how to become an Associated Person or Introducing Broker, and industry contact information.*
Center for Futures Education
    410 Erie Street
    PO Box 309
    Grove City, PA 16127
    Tel: 724-458-5860
    Email: info@thectr.com
    Web: http://www.thectr.com/

For information on the NASD Institute for Professional Development, contact:
National Association of Securities Dealers (NASD)
    33 Whitehall Street, 8th Floor
    New York, NY 10004
    Tel: 212-858-4020
    Web: http://www.nasd.com/

For information on registration and the National Commodities Futures Examination, contact:
National Futures Association
>200 West Madison Street, Suite 1600
>Chicago, IL 60606
>Tel: 800-621-3570
>Web: http://www.nfa.futures.org/

The Chicago Mercantile Exchange offers a wide variety of educational programs and materials, and general information on commodities careers through the Educational Resources section of its Web site. Particularly interesting is Do You Have a Future in Futures?, *an online career pamphlet that covers various careers in the industry.*
Chicago Mercantile Exchange
>30 South Wacker Drive
>Chicago, IL 60606
>Tel: 312-930-1000
>Email: edu@cme.com
>Web: http://www.cme.com

For a history of CBOT, and information on tours and educational programs, contact:
Chicago Board of Trade (CBOT)
>141 West Jackson Boulevard
>Chicago, IL 60604-2994
>Tel: 312-435-3500
>Web: http://www.cbot.com

For a general overview of options visit the Education section of the CBOE Web site:
The Chicago Board Options Exchange (CBOE)
>400 South LaSalle Street
>Chicago, IL 60605
>Web: http://www.cboe.com

The Educational section of the Philadelphia Board of Trade's Web site provides a glossary of terms, suggested reading, and an overview of the financial industry.
Philadelphia Board of Trade
>1900 Market Street
>Philadelphia, PA 19103-3584
>Tel: 215-496-5000
>Email: info@phlx.com
>Web: http://www.phlx.com

Visit the Web sites or contact the following exchanges for general background information about the field:

Coffee, Sugar & Cocoa Exchange, Inc.
4 World Trade Center
New York, NY 10048
Tel: 212-742-6000
Web: http://www.csce.com

MidAmerica Commodity Exchange
141 West Jackson Boulevard
Chicago, IL 60604
Tel: 312-341-3000
Web: http://www.midam.com

Minneapolis Grain Exchange
400 South 4th Street
130 Grain Exchange Building
Minneapolis, MN 55415
Tel: 800-827-4746
Email: info@mgex.com
Web: http://www.mgex.com

New York Futures Exchange
4 World Trade Center
New York, NY 10048
Tel: 212-938-2626
Web: http://www.nybot.com

New York Mercantile Exchange
NYMEX/COMEX
One North End Avenue
World Financial Center
New York, NY 10282-1101
Tel: 212-299-2000
Web: http://www.nymex.com

Computer Network Administrators

*Computer network administrators, or network specialists,
design, install, and support an organization's local area
network (LAN), wide area network (WAN), network seg-
ment, or Internet system. They maintain network hardware and software, analyze problems, and monitor the
network to ensure availability to system users.
Administrators also might plan, coordinate, and implement network security measures, including firewalls.*

The Job

Businesses use computer networks for several reasons. One important reason is that networks make it easy for many employees to share hardware
and software, as well as printers, faxes, and modems. For example, it would
be very expensive to buy individual copies of word-processing programs
for each employee in a company. By investing in a network version of the
software that all employees can access, companies can often save a lot of
money. Also, businesses that rely on databases for daily operations use networks to allow authorized personnel quick and easy access to the most
updated version of the database.

Networks vary greatly in size; even just two computers connected
together are considered a network. They can also be extremely large and
complex, involving hundreds of computer terminals in various geograph-
ical locations around the world. A good example of a large network is the
Internet, which is a system that allows people from every corner of the
globe to access millions of pieces of information about any subject under
the sun. Besides varying in size, networks are all at least slightly different
in terms of configuration, or what the network is designed to do; businesses customize networks to meet their specific needs. All networks,
regardless of size or configuration, experience problems. For example,
communications with certain equipment can break down, users might
need extra training or forget their passwords, back-up files may be lost, or

new software might need to be installed and configured. Whatever the crisis, computer network administrators must know the network system well enough to diagnose and fix the problem.

Computer network administrators or specialists may hold one or several networking responsibilities. The specific job duties assigned to one person depend on the nature and scope of the employer. For example, in a medium-size company that uses computers only minimally, a computer network specialist might be expected to do everything associated with the office computer system. In larger companies with more sophisticated computing systems, computer network administrators are likely to hold more narrow and better-defined responsibilities. The following descriptions highlight the different kinds of computer network administrators.

In the narrowest sense, computer network administrators are responsible for adding and deleting files to the network server, a centralized computer. Among other things, the server stores the software applications used by network users on a daily basis. Administrators update files from the database, electronic mail, and word-processing applications. They are also responsible for making sure that printing jobs run properly. This task entails telling the server where the printer is and establishing a printing queue, or line, designating which print jobs have priority.

Another duty of some network administrators is setting up user access. Since businesses store confidential information on the server, users typically have access to only a limited number of applications. Network administrators tell the computer who can use which programs and when they can use them. They create a series of passwords to secure the system against internal and external spying. They also troubleshoot problems and questions encountered by staff members.

In companies with large computer systems, *network security specialists* concentrate solely on system security. They set up and monitor user access and update security files as needed. For example, it is very important in universities that only certain administrative personnel have the ability to change student grades on the database. Network security specialists must protect the system from unauthorized grade changes. Network security specialists grant new passwords to users who forget them, record all nonauthorized entries, report unauthorized users to appropriate management, and change any files that have been tampered with. They also maintain security files with information about each employee.

Network control operators are in charge of all network communications, most of which operate over telephone lines or fiber optic cables.

When users encounter communications problems, they call the network control operator. A typical communications problem is when a user cannot send or receive files from other computers. Since users seldom have a high level of technical expertise on the network, the network control operator knows how to ask appropriate questions in user-friendly language to determine the source of the problem. If it is not a user error, the network control operator checks the accuracy of computer files, verifies that modems are functioning properly, and runs noise tests on the communications lines using special equipment. As with all network specialists, if the problem proves to be too difficult for the network control operator to resolve, he or she seeks help directly from the manufacturer or warranty company.

Network control operators also keep detailed records of the number of communications transactions made, the number and nature of network errors, and the methods used to resolve them. These records help them address problems as they arise in the future.

Network systems administrators that specialize in Internet technology are essential to its success. One of their responsibilities is to prepare servers for use and link them together, so others can place things on them. Under the supervision of the *Webmaster,* the systems administrator might set aside areas on a server for particular types of information, such as documents, graphics, or audio. At sites that are set up to handle secure credit card transactions, administrators are responsible for setting up the secure server that handles this job. They also monitor site traffic and take the necessary steps to ensure uninterrupted operation. In some cases, the solution is to provide additional space on the server. In others, the only solution might be to increase bandwidth by upgrading the telephone line linking the site to the Internet.

Requirements

High School

In high school, take as many courses as possible in computer science, mathematics, and science, which provide a solid foundation in computer basics and analytical-thinking skills. You should also practice your verbal and written communications skills in English and speech classes. Business courses are valuable in that they can give you an understanding of how important business decisions, especially those concerning investment in computer equipment, are made.

Postsecondary Training

Most network jobs require at least a bachelor's degree in computer science or computer engineering. More specialized positions require an advanced degree. People with a college education are more likely to deal with the theoretical aspects of computer networking and to be promoted to management positions. Opportunities in computer design, systems analysis, and computer programming, for example, are only open to college graduates. Individuals interested in this field should also pursue postsecondary training in network administration or network engineering.

"I believe that you cannot have enough education and that it should be an on-going thing," says Nancy Nelson, a network administrator at Baxter Healthcare Corporation in Deerfield, Illinois. "You can learn a lot on your own, but I think you miss out on a lot if you don't get the formal education. Most companies don't even look at a resume that doesn't have a degree. Keeping up with technology can be very rewarding."

Certification or Licensing

Besides the technical/vocational schools that offer courses related to computer networking, several major companies offer professionally taught courses and nationally recognized certification; chief among them are Novell and Microsoft. The Certified Network Professional program supports and complements the aforementioned vendor product certifications. Offered by The Network Professional Association, the program covers fundamental knowledge in client operating systems, microcomputer hardware platforms, network operating system fundamentals, protocols, and topologies. It requires that its students be certified in two specialty areas and have certifications in both.

Commercial postsecondary training programs are flexible. Individuals can complete their courses at their own pace, but must take all parts of the certification test within one year. Students can attend classes at any one of many educational sites around the country or can study on their own. Many students find certification exams difficult.

Other Requirements

Continuing education for any computer profession is crucial to success. Many companies require their computer network administrators to keep up to date on new technological advances by attending classes, workshops, and seminars throughout the year. Also, many companies and professional associations update network specialists through newsletters, other periodicals, and online bulletin boards.

Computer work is complex, detailed, and often very frustrating. Computer network administrators must be well organized and patient.

They should enjoy challenges and problem solving and should think logically. They must also be able to communicate complex ideas in simple terms. They have to be able to work well under pressure and deadlines. As any computer professional, network specialists should be naturally curious about the computing field; they must always be willing to learn more about new and different technologies.

Exploring

If you are interested in computer networking you should join computer clubs at school and community centers and surf the Internet or other online services. Ask your school administration about the possibility of working with the school system's network specialists for a day or longer. Parents' or friends' employers might also be a good place to find this type of opportunity.

If seeking part-time jobs, apply for those that include computer work. Though you will not find networking positions, any experience on computers will increase your general computing knowledge. In addition, once employed, you can actively seek exposure to the other computer functions in the business.

You might also try volunteering at local-area charities that use computer networks in their office. Since many charities have small budgets, they may offer more opportunities to gain experience with some of the simpler networking tasks. In addition, experiment by creating networks with your own computer, those of your friends, and any printers, modems, and faxes that you have access to.

Basically, you should play around on computers as much as possible. Read and learn from any resource you can, such as magazines, newsletters, and online bulletin boards.

Employers

Any company or organization that uses computer networks in its business employs network administrators. These include insurance companies, banks, financial institutions, health care organizations, federal and state governments, universities, and other corporations that rely on networking. Also, since smaller companies are moving to client-server models, more opportunities at almost any kind of business are becoming available.

Starting Out

There are several ways to obtain a position as a computer network specialist. If you are a student in a technical school or university, take advantage of the campus placement office. Check regularly for internship postings, job listings, and notices of on-campus recruitment. Placement offices are also valuable resources for resume tips and interviewing techniques. Internships and summer jobs with such corporations are always beneficial and provide experience that will give you the edge over your competition. General computer job fairs are also held throughout the year in larger cities.

There are many online career sites listed on the World Wide Web that post job openings, salary surveys, and current employment trends. The Web also has online publications that deal specifically with computer jobs. Interested students can obtain information from computer organizations, such as the IEEE Computer Society and The Network Professional Association.

When a job opportunity arises, you should send a cover letter and resume to the company promptly. Follow up your mailing with a phone call about one week later. If interested, the company recruiter will call to ask questions and possibly arrange an interview. The commercial sponsors of network certification, like Novell and Microsoft, also publish newsletters that list current job openings in the field. The same information is distributed through online bulletin boards and on the Internet as well. Otherwise, you can scan the classified ads in local newspapers and computer magazines or work with an employment agency to find such a position.

Individuals already employed but wishing to move into computer networking should investigate the possibility of tuition reimbursement from their employer for network certification. Many large companies have this type of program, which allows employees to train in a field that would benefit company operations. After successfully completing classes or certification, individuals are better qualified for related job openings in their own company and more likely to be hired into them.

Advancement

Advancement options for any computer professional are widely varied. Within the field of networking, administrators and specialists might be promoted to *network managers,* or they can get into network engineering. *Network engineers* design, test, and evaluate network systems, such as LAN, WAN, Internet, and other data communications systems. They also perform modeling, analysis, and planning. Network engineers might also research related products and make hardware and software recommendations.

Network specialists also have the option of going into a different area of computing. They can become computer programmers, systems analysts, software engineers, or multimedia professionals. All of these promotions require additional education and solid computer experience.

Earnings

Entry-level computer network administrators earn about $42,800 to $59,800 per year to start, according to Robert Half International. Mid-range salaries, for those with several years of experience and further training, are generally in the mid-sixties. High-range salaries in this field top off around $80,000. These salaries are reserved for individuals with solid experience, additional training, and demonstrated willingness to learn.

Most computer network administrators are employed by companies that offer the full range of benefits, including health insurance, paid vacation, and sick leave. In addition, many companies have tuition reimbursement programs for employees seeking to pursue education or professional certification.

Work Environment

Computer network administrators work indoors in a comfortable office environment. Their work is generally fast paced and can be frustrating. Some tasks, however, are routine and might get a little boring after awhile. But many times, network specialists are required to work under a lot of pressure. If the network goes down, for example, the company is losing money, and it is the network specialist's job to get it up and running as fast as possible. The specialist must be able to remember complicated relationships and many details accurately and quickly. They are also called on to deal effectively with the many complaints from network users.

When working on the installation of a new system, many network specialists are required to work overtime until it is fully operational. This usually includes long and frequent meetings. During initial operations of the system, some network specialists may be on-call during other shifts for when problems arise, or they may have to train network users during off hours.

One other potential source of frustration is communications with other employees. Network specialists deal every day with people who usually don't understand the system as well as they do. Network administrators must be able to communicate at different levels of understanding.

Outlook

The employment outlook for computer network administrators is expected to be faster than average through 2008, according to the U.S. Department of Labor. Network administrators are in high demand, particularly those with Internet experience.

"Technology is constantly changing," Nancy Nelson says. "It is hard to tell where it will lead in the future. I think that the Internet and all of its pieces will be the place to focus on."

As more and more companies discover the economic and convenience advantages linked to using computer networks at all levels of operations, the demand for well-trained network specialists will increase, and networking positions are likely to grow faster than average as those companies move from mainframe environments to client-server networks.

"I would say that as much as a person is willing to learn is really the amount of advancement opportunities that are open to them," notes Dan Creedon, a network administrator at Nesbitt Burns Securities in Chicago.

For More Information

Contact ACM for information on internships, student membership, and the ACM student magazine, Crossroads. *ACM also offers a student Web site at http://www.acm.org/membership/student/.*
Association for Computing Machinery (ACM)
    One Astor Plaza
    1515 Broadway
    New York, NY 10036
    Email: ACMHELP@acm.org
    Web: http://www.acm.org

For industry information, contact:
Network Professional Association
    195 C Street, Suite 250
    Tustin, CA 92780
    Email: npa@npa.org
    Web: http://www.npa.org

For information on scholarships, student membership, and the student newsletter, looking.forward, *contact:*
IEEE Computer Society
    1730 Massachusetts Avenue, NW
    Washington, DC 20036-1992
    Tel: 202-371-0101
    Web: http://www.computer.org

Computer Programmers

Computer programmers *work in the field of electronic data processing. They write instructions that tell computers what to do in a computer language, or code, that the computer understands.* Systems programmers *specialize in maintaining the general instructions that control an entire computer system. Maintenance tasks include giving computers instructions on how to allocate time to various jobs they receive from computer terminals and making sure that these assignments are performed properly.*

The Job

Broadly speaking, there are two types of computer programmers: systems programmers and *applications programmers.* Systems programmers maintain the instructions, called programs or software, that control the entire computer system, including both the central processing unit and the equipment with which it communicates, such as terminals, printers, and disk drives. Applications programmers write the software to handle specific jobs and may specialize as engineering and scientific programmers or as business programmers. Some of the latter specialists may be designated *chief business programmers,* who supervise the work of other business programmers.

Programmers are often given program specifications, prepared by systems analysts, which list in detail the steps the computer must follow in order to complete a given task. Programmers then code these instructions in a computer language the computer understands. In smaller companies, analysis and programming may be handled by the same person, called a *programmer-analyst.*

Before actually writing the computer program, a programmer must analyze the work request, understand the current problem and desired resolution, decide on an approach to the problem, and plan what the machine will have to do to produce the required results. Programmers prepare a flowchart to show the steps in sequence that the machine must make. They must pay attention to minute detail and instruct the machine in each step of the process.

These instructions are then coded in one of several programming languages, such as BASIC, COBOL, FORTRAN, PASCAL, RPG, CSP, or C++. When the program is completed, the programmer tests its working practicality by running it on simulated data. If the machine responds according to expectations, actual data will be fed into it and the program will be activated. If the computer does not respond as anticipated, the program will have to be debugged—that is, examined for errors that must be eliminated. Finally, the programmer prepares an instruction sheet for the computer operator who will run the program.

The programmer's job concerns both an overall picture of the problem at hand and the minute detail of potential solutions. Programmers work from two points of view: from that of the people who need certain results and from that of technological problem solving. The work is divided equally between meeting the needs of other people and comprehending the capabilities of the machines.

Electronic data systems involve more than just one machine. Depending upon the kind of system being used, the operation may require other machines such as printers or other peripherals. Introducing a new piece of equipment to an existing system often requires programmers to rewrite many programs.

Programmers may specialize in certain types of work, depending on the kind of problem to be solved and on the employer. Making a program for a payroll is, for example, very different from programming the study of structures of chemical compounds. Programmers who specialize in a certain field or industry generally have education or experience in that area before they are promoted to senior programming positions. *Information system programmers* specialize in programs for storing and retrieving physical science, engineering, or medical information; text analysis; and language, law, military, or library science data. As the information superhighway continues to grow, information system programmers have increased opportunities in online businesses, such as those of Lexis/Nexis, Westlaw, America Online, Microsoft, and many others.

Process control programmers develop programs for systems that control automatic operations for commercial and industrial enterprises, such as steelmaking, sanitation plants, combustion systems, computerized production testing, or automatic truck loading. *Numerical control tool pro-*

grammers program the tape that controls the machining of automatic machine tools.

Requirements

High School

In high school you should take any computer programming or computer science courses available. You should also concentrate on math, science, and schematic drawing courses, since these subjects directly prepare students for careers in computer programming.

Postsecondary Training

Most employers prefer their programmers to be college graduates. In the past, as the field was first taking shape, employers were known to hire people with some formal education and little or no experience but determination and aptitude to learn quickly. As the market becomes saturated with individuals wishing to break into this field, however, a college degree is becoming increasingly important. The U.S. Department of Labor reports that about 60 percent of computer programmers held a bachelor's degree or higher in 1998.

Many personnel officers administer aptitude tests to determine potential for programming work. Some employers send new employees to computer schools or in-house training sessions before they are considered qualified to assume programming responsibilities. Training periods may last as long as a few weeks, months, or even a year.

Many junior and community colleges also offer two-year associate's degree programs in data processing, computer programming, and other computer-related technologies.

Most four-year colleges and universities have computer science departments with a variety of computer-related majors, any of which could prepare a student for a career in programming. Employers who require a college degree often do not express a preference as to major field of study, although mathematics or computer science is highly favored. Other acceptable majors may be business administration, accounting, engineering, or physics. Entrance requirements for jobs with the government are much the same as those in private industry.

Certification or Licensing

Students who choose to obtain a two-year degree might consider becoming certified by the Institute for Certification of Computing Professionals. Although it is not required, certification may boost an individual's attractiveness to employers during the job search.

Other Requirements

Personal qualifications such as a high degree of reasoning ability, patience, and persistence, as well as aptitude for mathematics, are important for computer programmers. Some employers whose work is highly technical require that programmers be qualified in the area in which the firm or agency operates. Engineering firms, for example, prefer young people with an engineering background and are willing to train them in some programming techniques. For other firms, such as banks, consumer-level knowledge of the services that they offer may be sufficient background for incoming programmers.

Exploring

If you are interested in becoming a computer programmer, you might visit a large bank or insurance company in the community and seek an appointment to talk with one of the programmers on the staff. You may be able to visit the data processing center and see the machines in operation. You might also talk with a sales representative from one of the large manufacturers of data processing equipment and request whatever brochures or pamphlets the company publishes.

It is a good idea to start early and get some hands-on experience operating and programming a computer. A trip to the local library or bookstore is likely to turn up countless books on programming; this is one field where the resources to teach yourself are highly accessible and available for all levels of competency. Joining a computer club and reading professional magazines are other ways to become more familiar with this career field. In addition, you should start exploring the Internet, itself a great source of information about computer-related careers.

High school and college students who can operate a computer may be able to obtain part-time jobs in business computer centers or in some larger companies. Any computer experience will be helpful for future computer training.

Employers

Computer programmers work for manufacturing companies, data processing service firms, hardware and software companies, banks, insurance companies, credit companies, publishing houses, government agencies, and colleges and universities throughout the country. Many programmers are employed by businesses as consultants on a temporary or contractual basis.

Starting Out

You can look for an entry-level programming position in the same way as most other jobs; there is no special or standard point of entry into the field. Individuals with the necessary qualifications should apply directly to companies, agencies, or industries that have announced job openings through a school placement office, an employment agency, or the classified ads.

Students in two- or four-year degree programs should work closely with their schools' placement offices, since major local employers often list job openings exclusively with such offices.

If the market for programmers is particularly tight, you may want to obtain an entry-level job with a large corporation or computer software firm, even if the job does not include programming. As jobs in the programming department open up, current employees in other departments are often the first to know, and are favored over nonemployees during the interviewing process. Getting a foot in the door in this way has proven to be successful for many programmers.

Advancement

Programmers are ranked—according to education, experience, and level of responsibility—as junior or senior programmers. After programmers have attained the highest available programming position, they can choose to make one of several career moves in order to be promoted still higher.

Some programmers are more interested in the analysis aspect of computing than the actual charting and coding of programming. They often acquire additional training and experience in order to prepare themselves for promotion to positions as systems programmers or systems analysts. These individuals have the added responsibility of working with upper management to define equipment and cost guidelines for a specific project. They perform only broad programming tasks, leaving most of the detail work to programmers.

Other programmers become more interested in administration and management and may wish to become heads of programming departments. They tend to be more people-oriented and enjoy leading others to excellence. As the level of management responsibilities increases, the amount of technical work performed decreases, so management positions are not for everyone.

Still other programmers may branch out into different technical areas, such as total computer operations, hardware design, and software or network engineering. With experience, they may be placed in charge of the data systems center. They may also decide to go to work for a consulting company, work that generally pays extremely well.

Programming provides a solid background in the computer industry. Experienced programmers enjoy a wide variety of possibilities for career advancement. The hardest part for programmers usually is deciding exactly what they want to do.

Earnings

According to the National Association of Colleges and Employers, the average 1999 starting salary for college graduates employed in the private sector was about $40,800. The U.S. Department of Labor reports that median annual earnings for computer programmers were $47,550 in 1998. The lowest 10 percent of programmers earned $27,760, while the highest 10 percent earned more than $88,730 annually.

Programmers in the West and the Northeast are generally paid more than those in the South and Midwest. This is because most big computer companies are located in the Silicon Valley in northern California or in the state of Washington, where Microsoft, a major employer of programmers, has its headquarters. Also, some industries, like public utilities and data processing service firms, tend to pay their programmers higher wages than do other types of employers, such as banks and schools.

Most programmers receive the customary paid vacation and sick leave and are included in such company benefits as group insurance and retirement benefit plans.

Work Environment

Most programmers work in pleasant office conditions, since computers require an air-conditioned, dust-free environment. Programmers perform most of their duties in one primary location but may be asked to travel to other computing sites on occasion.

The average programmer works between 35 and 40 hours weekly. In some job situations, the programmer may have to work nights or weekends on short notice. This might happen when a program is going through its trial runs, for example, or when there are many demands for additional services.

Outlook

Employment opportunities for computer programmers should increase faster than the average through 2008, according to the U.S. Department of Labor. Employment growth will be strong because businesses, scientific organizations, government agencies, and schools continue to look for new applications for computers and to make improvements in software already in use. Also, there is a need to develop complex operating programs that can use higher-level computer languages and can network with other computer equipment and systems.

Job applicants with the best chances of employment will be college graduates with a knowledge of several programming languages, especially newer ones used for computer networking and database management. In addition, the best applicants will have some training or experience in an applied field such as accounting, science, engineering, or management. Competition for jobs will be heavier among graduates of two-year data processing programs and among people with equivalent experience or with less training. Since this field is constantly changing, programmers should stay abreast of the latest technology to remain competitive.

For More Information

For more information about careers in computer programming, contact:
Association for Computing Machinery
    One Astor Plaza
    1515 Broadway
    New York, NY 10036
    Tel: 800-342-6626
    Email: ACMHELP@acm.org
    Web: http://www.acm.org
    and http://www.acm.org/membership/student/

Association of Information Technology Professionals
    315 South Northwest Highway, Suite 200
    Park Ridge, IL 60068-4278
    Email: 70430.35@compuserve.com
    Web: http://www.aitp.org

For information on certification programs, contact:
Institute for Certification of Computing Professionals
    2200 East Devon Avenue, Suite 247
    Des Plaines, IL 60018
    Email: 74040.3722@compuserve.com
    Web: http://www.iccp.org

Computer Systems/ Programmer Analysts

Overview

*Computer systems/programmer analysts **first analyze the computing needs of a business and then design a new system or upgrade an old system to meet those needs. The position can be split between two people, the** systems programmer **and the** systems analyst, **but is frequently held by just one person who oversees the work from beginning to end.***

The Job

Businesses invest hundreds of thousands of dollars in computer systems to make their operations more efficient and thus more profitable. As older systems become obsolete, businesses are also faced with the task of replacing them or upgrading them with new technology. Computer systems/programmer analysts plan and develop new computer systems or upgrade existing systems to meet changing business needs. They also install, modify, and maintain functioning computer systems. The process of choosing and implementing a computer system is similar for programmer analysts who work for very different employers. However, specific decisions in terms of hardware and software differ depending on the industry.

The first stage of the process involves meeting with management and users in order to discuss the problem at hand. For example, a company's accounting system might be slow, unreliable, and generally outdated. During many hours of meetings, systems/programmer analysts and management discuss various options, including commercial software, hardware upgrades, and customizing possibilities that may solve the problems. At the end of the discussions, which may last as long as several weeks or months, the programmer analyst defines the specific system goals as agreed upon by participants.

Next, systems/programmer analysts engage in highly analytic and logical activities. They use tools like structural analysis, data modeling, mathematics, and cost accounting to determine which computers, including hardware and software and peripherals, will be required to meet the goals of the project. They must consider the trade-offs between extra efficiency and speed and increased costs. Weighing the pros and cons of each additional system feature is an important factor in system planning. Whatever preliminary decisions are made must be supported by mathematical and financial evidence.

As the final stage of the planning process, systems/programmer analysts prepare reports and formal presentations to be delivered to management. Reports must be written in clear, concise language that business professionals, who are not necessarily technical experts, can understand thoroughly. Formal presentations in front of groups of various sizes are often required as part of the system proposal.

If the system or the system upgrades are approved, equipment is purchased and installed. Then, the programmer analysts get down to the real technical work so that all the different computers and peripherals function well together. They prepare specifications, diagrams, and other programming structures and, perhaps using CASE (computer-aided systems engineering) technology, they write the new or upgraded programming code. If they work solely as systems analysts, it is at this point that they hand over all of their information to the systems programmer so that he or she can begin to write the programming code.

Systems design and programming involves defining the files and records to be accessed by the system, outlining the processing steps, and suggesting formats for output that meet the needs of the company. User-friendliness of the front-end applications is extremely important for user productivity. Therefore, programmer analysts must be able to envision how nontechnical system users view their on-screen work. Systems/programmer analysts might also specify security programs that allow only authorized personnel access to certain files or groups of files.

As the programming is written, programmer analysts set up test runs of various parts of the system, making sure each step of the way that major goals are reached. Once the system is up and running, problems, or bugs, begin to pop up. Programmer analysts are responsible for debugging. They must isolate the problem and review the hundreds of lines of programming commands to determine where the mistake is located. Then they must enter the correct command or code and recheck the program.

Depending on the employer, some systems/programmer analysts might be involved with computer networking. Network communication programs tell two or more computers or peripherals how to work with each other. When a system is composed of equipment from various manufacturers, networking is essential for smooth system functioning. For example, shared printers have to know how to order print jobs as they come in from various terminals. Some programmer analysts write the code that establishes printing queues. Others might be involved in user training since they know the software applications well. They might also customize commercial software programs to meet the needs of their company.

Many programmer analysts become specialized in an area of business, science, or engineering. They seek education and further on-the-job training in these areas to develop expertise. They may therefore attend special seminars, workshops, and classes designed for their needs. This extra knowledge allows them to develop a deeper understanding of the computing problems specific to the business or industry.

Requirements

High School

A bachelor's degree in computer science is a minimum requirement for systems/programmer analysts. If you are interested in this career, in high school you should take as many math, science, and computer classes as possible. These courses provide a foundation of basic concepts and encourage the development of analytic and logical thinking skills. Since programmer analysts do a lot of proposal writing that may or may not be technical in nature, English classes are valuable as well. Speech classes will help prepare you for making formal presentations to management and clients.

Postsecondary Training

Course work in preparation for this field includes math, computer programming, science, and logic. Several years of related work experience, including knowledge of programming languages, are often necessary as well. For some very high-level positions, an advanced degree in a specific computer subfield may be required. Also, depending on the employer, proficiency in business, science, or engineering may be necessary.

Certification or Licensing

Some programmer analysts pursue certification through the Institute for Certification of Computing Professionals. In particular, they take classes and exams to become certified systems professionals (CSPs). Certification is voluntary and is an added credential for job hunters. CSPs have achieved a recognized level of knowledge and experience in principles and practices related to systems.

Other Requirements

Successful systems/programmer analysts demonstrate strong analytic skills and enjoy the challenges of problem solving. They are able to understand problems that exist on many levels, from a very technical problem to a more practical, business-oriented one. They can visualize complicated and abstract relationships between computer hardware and software and are good at matching needs to equipment.

Programmer analysts have to be flexible as well. They routinely deal with many different kinds of people, from management to data entry clerks. Therefore, they must be knowledgeable in a lot of functional areas of the company. They should be able to talk to management about cost-effective solutions, to programmers about detailed coding, and to clerks about user-friendliness of the applications.

As is true for all computer professionals, systems/programmer analysts must be able to learn about new technologies quickly. They should be naturally curious about keeping up on cutting-edge developments; keeping up can be time-consuming. Furthermore, they are often so busy at their jobs that staying in the know is done largely on their own time.

Exploring

If you are interested, you have several options to learn more about what it is like to be a computer systems/programmer analyst. You can spend a day with a working professional in this field in order to experience first-hand a typical day. Career days of this type can usually be arranged through school guidance counselors or the public relations manager of local corporations.

Strategy games, including chess, played with friends or school clubs are a good way to put your analytic thinking skills to use while having fun. Commercial games range in themes from war simulations to world historical development. When choosing a game, the key is to make sure it relies on qualities similar to those used by programmer analysts.

Lastly, you should become a computer hobbyist and learn everything you can about computers by working and playing with them on a daily basis. Surfing the Internet regularly, as well as reading trade magazines, will also be helpful. You might also want to try hooking up a mini system at home or school, configuring terminals, printers, modems, and other peripherals into a coherent system. This activity requires a fair amount of knowledge and so should be supervised by a professional.

Employers

Computer systems/programmer analysts work for all types of firms and organizations that do their work on computers. Such companies may include manufacturing companies, data processing service firms, hardware and software companies, banks, insurance companies, credit companies, publishing houses, government agencies, and colleges and universities. Many programmer analysts are employed by businesses as consultants on a temporary or contractual basis.

Starting Out

Since systems/programmer analysts typically have at least some experience in a computer-related job, most are hired into these positions from lower-level ones within the same company. For example, programmers, software engineering technicians, and network and database administrators all gain valuable computing experience that can be put to good use at a systems job. Alternatively, individuals who acquire expertise in systems programming and analysis while in other jobs may want to work with a headhunter to find the right systems positions for them. Also, trade magazines, newspapers, and employment agencies regularly feature job openings in this field. Another source of job information is Career Mosaic on the World Wide Web. Career Mosaic is a service that makes access to various companies' job listings easier and faster.

Students in four-year degree programs should work closely with their schools' placement offices. Companies regularly work through such offices in order to find the best-qualified graduates. Since it may be difficult to find a job as a programmer analyst to begin with, it is important for students to consider their long-term potential within a certain company. The chance for promotion into a systems job can make lower-level jobs more appealing, at least in the short run. The educational reimbursement policy of the company is another important consideration, since it can enable individuals to achieve the educational requirements of systems jobs inexpensively.

For those individuals already employed in a computer-related job but wanting to get into systems programming and analysis, additional formal education is a good idea. Some employers without educational policies may be willing to pay for such training if it could directly benefit the business.

Advancement

Systems/programmer analysts already occupy a relatively high level technical job. Promotion, therefore, usually occurs in one of two directions. First, programmer analysts can be put in charge of increasingly larger and more complex systems. Instead of concentrating on a local system—for example, the corporate services systems—an analyst can oversee all company systems and networks. This kind of technically based promotion can also put systems/programmer analysts into other areas of computing. With the proper experience and additional training, they can get into database or network management and design, software engineering, or even quality assurance.

The other direction in which programmer analysts can go is managerial. Depending on the position sought, formal education—either a bachelor's degree in business or a master's in business administration—may be required. As more administrative duties are added, more technical ones are taken away. Therefore, programmer analysts who enjoy the technical aspect of their work more than anything else may not want to pursue this advancement track. Excellent computing managers have both a solid background in various forms of computing and a good grasp of what it takes to run a department. Also, having the vision to see how technology will change in the short and long terms, and how those changes will affect the industry concerned, is a quality of a good manager.

Earnings

According to the U.S. Department of Labor, annual salaries for systems/programmer analysts averaged about $52,180 in 1998. Fifty percent earned from $40,570 to $74,180 a year. Salaries are slightly higher in geographic areas where many computer companies are clustered, like northern California and Seattle, Washington. According to the National Association of Colleges and Employers, programmer analysts with a bachelor's degree earned an average of $39,722 a year; those holding a master's degree or higher earned from $44,734 to $63,367 a year.

Most programmer analysts receive health insurance, paid vacation, and sick leave. Some employers offer tuition reimbursement programs and in-house computer training workshops.

Work Environment

Computer systems/programmer analysts work in a comfortable office environment. If they work as consultants, they may travel frequently.

Otherwise, travel is limited to trade shows, seminars, and visitations to vendors for demonstrations. They might also visit other businesses to observe their systems in action.

Programmer analysts usually work 40-hour weeks and enjoy the regular holiday schedule of days off. However, as deadlines for system installation, upgrades, and debugging approach, they are often required to work overtime in order to meet them. Extra compensation for overtime hours may come in the form of time-and-a-half pay or compensatory time off, depending on the precise nature of the employee's duties, company policy, and state law. If the employer operates off-shifts, programmer analysts may be on-call to address any problems that might arise at any time of the day or night. This is relatively rare in the service sector but more common in manufacturing, heavy industry, and data processing firms.

Computer systems programming and analysis is very detailed work. The tiniest error can cause major system disruptions, which can be a great source of frustration. Systems/programmer analysts must be prepared to deal with this frustration and be able to work well under pressure.

Outlook

The U.S. Department of Labor predicts that the occupation of computer systems/programmer analyst will be one of the three fastest growing careers through 2008. Increases are mainly a product of the growing number of businesses that rely extensively on computers. When businesses automate, their daily operations depend on the capacity of their computer systems to perform at desired levels. The development of new technology and the need for businesses to network their information will add to the demand for qualified programmer analysts. Businesses will rely increasingly on systems/programmer analysts to make the right purchasing decisions and to keep systems running smoothly.

Many computer manufacturers are beginning to expand the range of services they offer to business clients. In the years to come, they may hire many systems/programmer analysts to work as consultants on a per-project basis with a potential client. These workers would perform essentially the same duties, with the addition of extensive follow-up maintenance. They would analyze business needs and suggest proper systems to answer them. In addition, more and more independent consulting firms are hiring systems/programmer analysts to perform the same tasks.

Programmer analysts with advanced degrees in computer science, management information systems, or computer engineering, will be in great demand. MBAs with emphasis in information systems will also be highly desirable.

For More Information

For more information about systems/programmer analyst positions, contact the following organizations:

Association for Systems Management
> 1433 West Bagley Road
> PO Box 38370
> Cleveland, OH 44138
> Tel: 216-234-2930

Association of Information Technology Professionals
> 315 South Northwest Highway, Suite 200
> Park Ridge, IL 60068-4278
> Tel: 800-224-9371
> Email: 70430.35@compuserve.com
> Web: http://www.aitp.org

For information on certification programs, contact:
Institute for Certification of Computing Professionals
> 2200 East Devon Avenue, Suite 247
> Des Plaines, IL 60018
> Tel: 800-843-8422
> Email: 74040.3722@compuserve.com
> Web: http://www.iccp.org

Database
Specialists

Overview

Database specialists *design, install, update, modify, maintain, and repair computer database systems. They consult with other management officials to discuss computer equipment purchases, determine requirements for various computer programs, and allocate access to the computer system to users. They might also direct training of personnel who use company databases regularly.*

The Job

Database specialists come in many varieties, depending on the needs of the organizations that employ them. In large businesses there may be several database specialists who focus on specific aspects of a company's databases. In a smaller organization, one person may wear all the database hats. Database specialists are also known as *database administrators, database managers,* or *information systems managers.* Database specialists rely on their knowledge of database management to code, test, and install new databases. They review proposals for changes in existing database systems and evaluate how well such changes would work on a daily basis. They are also responsible for overseeing the daily operations of the computer systems. These tasks include ensuring that information is being entered and encoded properly by data entry clerks, that various processing programs are retrieving the right information, and that the systems are not experiencing major problems.

Database specialists are responsible for the flow of computer information within an organization. They make major decisions concerning computer purchases, system designs, and personnel training. Their duties combine general management ability with a detailed knowledge of computer programming and systems analysis.

The specific responsibilities of a database specialist are determined by the size and type of employer. For example, a database manager for a telephone company may develop a system for billing customers, while a database manager for a large store may develop a system for keeping track of merchandise in stock. In all cases, most database specialists have a thorough knowledge and understanding of the company's computer operations.

A database specialist's responsibilities can be grouped into three main areas: planning what type of computer system a company needs; implementing and managing the system; and supervising computer room personnel.

To adequately plan a computer system, database specialists must have extensive knowledge of the latest computer technology and the specific needs of their company. Database specialists meet with other high-ranking company officials, such as the president or vice president, and together they decide how to apply the available technology to their company's needs. Decisions include what type of hardware and software to order and how the data should be stored. Database specialists must be aware of the cost of the proposed computer system as well as the budget within which the company is operating. Long-term planning is also important. Database managers must ensure that the computer system can process not only the existing level of computer information received, but also the anticipated load and type of information the company could receive in the future. Such planning is vitally important since, even for small companies, computer systems can cost several hundred thousand dollars.

Database managers must be familiar with accounting principles and mathematical formulas in developing proposals. It is not unusual for a database manager to modify an existing computer system or develop a whole new system based on a company's needs and resources.

Implementing and managing a computer system entails a variety of administrative tasks. Database administrators decide how to organize and store the information files so only the appropriate users gain access to them. In addition, program files must be coded for efficient retrieval. Scheduling access to the computer is another vital administrative function. Sometimes, database administrators work with representatives from all the departments to create a schedule. The administrator prioritizes needs and monitors usage so that each department can do its work. All computer usage must be documented and filed away for future reference.

Safeguarding the computer operations is another important responsibility of database specialists. They must make plans in case a computer system fails or malfunctions so that the information stored in the computer is not lost. A duplication of computer files may be a part of this emergency planning. A backup system must also be employed so that the company can continue to process information. Increasingly, database specialists must also safeguard a system so that only authorized personnel have access to certain information. Computerized information may be of vital importance to a company, and database specialists ensure that it does not fall into the wrong hands.

Implementation of a computer operation often involves coordinating the integration of many complex computers into a single system. As an operation grows, this may require the modification of the system.

Database managers must be able to analyze a computer operation and decide if it is operating at top efficiency. They must be able to recognize equipment or personnel problems and adjust the system accordingly. They are often working with an operation that processes millions of bits of information at a huge cost. This demands accuracy and efficiency in decision-making and problem-solving abilities.

Requirements

High School

Prior experience with computers is essential to obtaining a position as a database specialist. If you are interested in this field you should take computer programming courses and any electronics or other technical courses that provide understanding of how a computer operates. Mathematics, science, and accounting courses are also desirable. English and speech courses are a good way for you to hone your written and verbal communications skills.

Postsecondary Training

A bachelor's degree is often a prerequisite to be hired as a computer professional. Sometimes, if the candidate shows exceptional experience in the computer field, an associate's degree in a computer-related technology from a technical or vocational school is sufficient to fulfill education requirements. Course work may include classes in electronics, computer hardware and software, physics, mathematics, schematic reading, and basic programming. Many employers prefer their database administrators to have a background in computer science, information science, computer information systems, or data processing.

Promotion from entry-level administrator jobs to managerial positions will require a bachelor's degree in one of the following: computer science, information science, computer information systems, data processing, or business administration. Sometimes, work experience within the company can compensate for a lack of more formal education. Courses in a bachelor's degree program usually include data processing, systems analysis methods, more detailed software and hardware concepts, management principles, and information systems planning. Many businesses, especially larger companies, prefer database managers to have a master's degree in computer science or business administration.

Certification or Licensing

Some database specialists become certified for jobs in the computer field by passing an examination given by the Institute for Certification of Computing Professionals (ICCP). The examination is offered in selected cities throughout the United States every year. For further information on certification, contact the ICCP at the address given at the end of this article.

Other Requirements

Experience as a computer programmer or systems analyst is also desirable. Those familiar with programming language will be in demand. Individuals interested in working almost exclusively in one industry, such as banking, for example, should acquire as much knowledge as possible about that specific field in addition to their extensive computer training. General knowledge in database administration might not prepare an individual for working in a bank unless he or she also understands basic bank operations and goals. With an understanding of both fields of knowledge, individuals are more easily able to apply computer technology to the specific needs of the company.

Exploring

High school computer clubs offer a good forum for learning about computers and meeting others interested in the field. Some businesses offer part-time work or summer internships in their computer departments for qualified students. In addition, there are training programs, such as those offered at summer camps, that teach computer literacy during an intensive three- to six-week period. You might also ask your school administrators about databases used by the school and try to interview any database specialists working in or for the school system. Similar attempts could be made with charities in your local area that make use of computer databases for membership and client records as well as mailing lists.

Employers

Database specialists work for investment companies, telecommunications firms, banks, insurance companies, publishing houses, and a host of other large and midsize businesses and nonprofit organizations. There are also many opportunities with the federal, state, and city governments.

Teaching, whether as a consultant or at a university or community college, is another option for individuals with high levels of experience.

Starting Out

Since at least an associate's degree is needed to obtain a position in this field, most database professionals work closely with their school's placement office to obtain information about job openings and interviews. Interested individuals might also scan the classified ads or work with temporary agencies to find entry-level and midlevel positions. Some applicants with extensive on-the-job computer training may be promoted to this position without a degree, but as the field gets more sophisticated, a college degree will continue to be the most dependable means of entering the profession.

College internships or co-op programs are good ways to gain credible work experience and meet valuable contacts for the future. Many businesses favor applicants already familiar with company standards and goals.

Advancement

Skilled database specialists have excellent advancement opportunities. As specialists acquire education and develop solid work experience, advancement will take the form of more responsibilities and higher wages. Database administrators are promoted into database design and management positions. A database specialist at a small company that relies heavily on database technology may move to an upper-level position such as vice president of the firm or may move to a better-paying, more challenging database position at a larger company. Superior database managers at larger companies may also be promoted to executive positions. Some successful database managers become high-paid consultants or start their own businesses.

Earnings

Earnings vary with the size and type of organization and a person's experience, education, and job responsibilities. According to the *Occupational Outlook Handbook,* median annual earnings for database specialists were $47,980 in 1998. The lowest 10 percent earned less than $26,690, while the highest 10 percent earned more than $86,200. Database administrators, depending on the company and the degree of responsibility, could easily earn more. Consultants working for major computer companies usually earn higher salaries.

Work Environment

Database specialists work in modern offices, usually located next to the computer room. Most duties are performed at a computer on the individual's desk. Travel is occasionally required for conferences and visits to affiliated database locations.

Database specialists work a regular 40-hour week, but higher-level positions sometimes require longer hours, especially when major system changes are being implemented. Emergencies may also require specialists to work overtime or long hours without a break, sometimes through the night.

Outlook

The use of computers and database systems in almost all business creates tremendous opportunities for well-qualified database personnel. Database specialists and computer support specialists are predicted by the U.S. Department of Labor to be the two fastest growing occupations through the year 2008.

Employment opportunities for database specialists should be best in large urban areas because of the multitudes of businesses that have computer systems. Since smaller communities are also rapidly developing significant job opportunities, skilled workers can pick from a wide range of jobs throughout the country. Those with the best education and the most experience in computer systems and personnel management will find the best job prospects.

For More Information

For general information on career opportunities or information regarding one of their 300 student chapters, contact:
Association of Information Technology Professionals
315 South Northwest Highway, Suite 200
Park Ridge, IL 60068-4278
Tel: 800-224-9371
Email: 70430.35@compuserve.com
Web: http://www.aitp.org

For more information about computer certification, contact:
Institute for Certification of Computing Professionals
2200 East Devon Avenue, Suite 247
Des Plaines, IL 60018
Tel: 800-843-8422
Web: http://www.iccp.org

Electrical and Electronics Engineers

Overview

Electrical engineers *apply their knowledge of the sciences to working with equipment that produces and distributes electricity, such as generators, transmission lines, and transformers. They also design, develop, and manufacture electric motors, electrical machinery, and ignition systems for automobiles, aircraft, and other engines.*

Electronics engineers *are more concerned with devices made up of electronic components such as integrated circuits and microprocessors. They design, develop, and manufacture products such as computers, telephones, and radios. Electronics engineering is a subfield of electrical engineering, and both types of engineers are often referred to as electrical engineers.*

The Job

Because electrical and electronics engineering is such a diverse field, there are numerous divisions and departments within which engineers work. In fact, the discipline reaches nearly every other field of applied science and technology. In general, electrical and electronics engineers use their knowledge of the sciences in the practical applications of electrical energy. They concern themselves with things as large as atom smashers and as small as microchips. They are involved in the invention, design, construction, and operation of electrical and electronic systems and devices of all kinds.

The work of electrical and electronics engineers touches almost every niche of our lives. Think of the things around you that have been designed, manufactured, maintained, or in any other way affected by electrical energy: the lights in a room, cars on the road, televisions, stereo systems, telephones, your doctor's blood-pressure reader, computers. When you start to think in these terms, you will discover that the electrical engineer has in some way had a hand in science, industry, commerce, entertainment, and even art.

The list of specialties that engineers are associated with reads like an alphabet of scientific titles—from acoustics, speech, and signal processing; to electromagnetic compatibility; geoscience and remote sensing; lasers and electro-optics; robotics; ultrasonics, ferroelectrics, and frequency control; to vehicular technology. As evident in this selected list, engineers are apt to specialize in what interests them, such as communications, robotics, or automobiles.

As mentioned earlier, electrical engineers focus on high-power generation of electricity and how it is transmitted for use in lighting homes and powering factories. They are also concerned with how equipment is designed and maintained and how communications are transmitted via wire and airwaves. Some are involved in the design and construction of power plants and the manufacture and maintenance of industrial machinery.

Electronics engineers work with smaller-scale applications, such as how computers are wired, how appliances work, or how electrical circuits are used in an endless number of applications. They may specialize in computers, industrial equipment and controls, aerospace equipment, or biomedical equipment.

Tom Busch is an electrical engineer for the U.S. government. He works at the Naval Surface Warfare Center, Crane Division, and much of his work involves testing equipment that will be used on the Navy's ships. "We get equipment that government contractors have put together and test it to make sure it is functioning correctly before it goes out to the fleet," he says. "The type of equipment we test might be anything from navigation to propulsion to communications equipment." Although much of his work currently focuses on testing, Tom also does design work. "We do some software design and also design circuits that go in weapons systems," he says.

Design and testing are only two of several categories in which electrical and electronics engineers may find their niche. Others include research and development, production, field service, sales and marketing, and teaching. In addition, even within each category there are divisions of labor.

Researchers concern themselves mainly with issues that pertain to potential applications. They conduct tests and perform studies to evaluate fundamental problems involving such things as new materials and chemical interactions. Those who work in design and development adapt the researchers' findings to actual practical applications. They devise functioning devices and draw up plans for their efficient production, using computer-aided design and engineering (CAD/CAE) tools. For a typical product such as a television, this phase usually takes up to 18 months to accomplish. For other products, particularly those that utilize developing technology, this phase can take as long as 10 years or more.

Production engineers have perhaps the most hands-on tasks in the field. They are responsible for the organization of the actual manufacture of whatever electric product is being made. They take care of materials and machinery, schedule technicians and assembly workers, and make sure that standards are met and products are quality-controlled. These engineers must have access to the best tools for measurement, materials handling, and processing.

After electrical systems are put in place, *field service engineers* must act as the liaison between the manufacturer or distributor and the client. They ensure the correct installation, operation, and maintenance of systems and products for both industry and individuals. In the sales and marketing divisions, engineers stay abreast of customer needs in order to evaluate potential applications, and they advise their companies of orders and effective marketing. A *sales engineer* would contact a client interested in, say, a certain type of microchip for its automobile electrical system controls. He or she would learn about the client's needs and report back to the various engineering teams at his or her company. During the manufacture and distribution of the product, the sales engineer would continue to communicate information between company and client until all objectives were met.

All engineers must be taught their skills, and so it is important that some remain involved in academia. *Professors* usually teach a portion of the basic engineering courses as well as classes in the subjects that they specialize in. Conducting personal research is generally an ongoing task for professors in addition to the supervision of student work and student research. A part of the teacher's time is also devoted to providing career and academic guidance to students.

Whatever type of project an engineer works on, he or she is likely to have a certain amount of desk work. Writing status reports and communicating with clients and others who are working on the same project are examples of the paperwork that most engineers are responsible for. Tom says that the amount of time he spends doing desk work varies from project to project. "Right now, I probably spend about half of my time in the lab and half at my desk," he says. "But it varies, really. Sometimes, I'm hardly in the lab at all; other times, I'm hardly at my desk."

Requirements

High School

Electrical and electronics engineers must have a solid educational background. The discipline is based on much in the applied sciences but requires a clear understanding of practical applications. To prepare for college, high school students should take classes in algebra, trigonometry, calculus, biology, physics, chemistry, computer science, word processing, English, and social studies. According to Tom, business classes are also a good idea. "It wouldn't hurt to get some business understanding—and computer skills are tremendously important for engineers, as well," he says. Students who are planning to pursue studies beyond a bachelor of science degree will also need to take a foreign language. It is recommended that students aim for honors-level courses.

Postsecondary Training

Tom's educational background includes a bachelor of science degree in electrical engineering. Other engineers might receive similar degrees in electronics, computer engineering, or another related science. Numerous colleges and universities offer electrical, electronics, and computer engineering programs. Because the programs vary from one school to another, you should explore as many schools as possible to determine which program is most suited to your academic and personal interests and needs. Most engineering programs have strict admission requirements and require students to have excellent academic records and top scores on national college-entrance examinations. Competition can be fierce for some programs, and high school students are encouraged to apply early.

Many students go on to receive a master of science degree in a specialization of their choice. This usually takes an additional two years of study beyond a bachelor's program. Some students pursue a master's degree immediately upon completion of a bachelor's degree. Other students, however, gain work experience first and then take graduate-level courses on a part-time basis while they are employed. A doctoral degree, or Ph.D., is also available. It generally requires four years of study and research beyond the bachelor's degree and is usually completed by people interested in research or teaching.

By the time you reach college, it is wise to be considering which type of engineering specialty you might be interested in. In addition to the core engineering curriculum (advanced mathematics, physical science, engineering science, mechanical drawing, computer applications), students will begin to choose from the following types of courses: circuits and electronics, signals and systems, digital electronics and computer architecture, electromagnetic waves, systems, and machinery, communications, and statistical mechanics.

Other Requirements

To be a good electrical or electronics engineer, you should have strong problem-solving abilities, mathematical and scientific aptitudes, and the willingness to learn throughout one's career. According to Tom, a curiosity for how things work is also important. "I think you have to like to learn about things," he says. "I also think it helps to be kind of creative, to like to make things."

Most engineers work on teams with other professionals, and the ability to get along with others is essential. In addition, strong communications skills are needed. Engineers need to be able to write reports and give oral presentations.

Exploring

People who are interested in the excitement of electricity can tackle experiments such as building a radio or central processing unit of a computer. Special assignments can also be researched and supervised by teachers. Joining a science club, such as the Junior Engineering Technical Society (JETS), can provide hands-on activities and opportunities to explore scientific topics in depth. Student members can join competitions and design structures that exhibit scientific know-how. Reading trade publications, such as the *JETS Report,* are other ways to learn about the engineering field. This magazine includes articles on engineering-related careers and club activities.

Students can also learn more about electrical and electronics engineering by attending a summer camp or academic program that focuses on scientific projects as well as recreational activities. For example, the Delphian School in Oregon holds summer sessions for high school students. Students are involved in leadership activities and special interests such as computers. Sports and wilderness activities are also offered. Summer programs such as the one offered by the Michigan Technological University focus on career exploration in computers, electronics, and robotics. This academic program for high school students also offers arts guidance, wilderness events, and other recreational activities. (For further information on clubs and programs, write to the sources listed at the end of this article.)

Employers

Most electrical and electronics engineers work in industry, often for design and manufacturing companies or consulting agencies. Others, like Tom, work for the federal government, as teachers in engineering schools and programs, and in research. Some work as private consultants.

Starting Out

Many students begin to research companies that they are interested in working for during their last year of college or even before. It is possible to research companies using many resources, such as company directories and annual reports, available at public libraries. For example, *The Career Guide, Dun's Employment Opportunity Directory* lists companies that are employing people in electrical/electronics engineering positions, as well as other careers. It gives brief company profiles, describes employment opportunities within the company, and provides addresses to which applicants can write.

Employment opportunities can be found through a variety of sources. Many engineers are recruited by companies while they are still in college. This is what happened to Tom. "I was interviewed while I was still on campus, and I was hired for the job before I graduated," he says. Other companies have internship, work-study, or cooperative education programs from which they hire students who are still in college. Students who have participated in these program often receive permanent job offers through these companies, or they may obtain useful contacts that can lead to a job interview or offer. Some companies use employment agencies and state employment offices. Companies may also advertise positions through advertisements in newspapers and trade publications. In addition, many newsletters and associations post job listings on the Internet.

Interested applicants can also apply directly to a company they are interested in working for. A letter of interest and resume can be sent to the director of engineering or the head of a specific department. One may also apply to the personnel or human resources departments.

Advancement

Engineering careers usually offer many avenues for advancement. An engineer straight out of college will usually take a job as an entry-level engineer and advance to higher positions after acquiring some job experience and technical skills. Engineers with strong technical skills who show leadership ability and good communications skills may move into positions that involve supervising teams of engineers and making sure they are working efficiently. Engineers can advance from these positions to that of a *chief engineer.* The chief engineer usually oversees all projects and has authority over project managers and managing engineers.

Many companies provide structured programs to train new employees and prepare them for advancement. These programs usually rely heavily on formal training opportunities such as in-house development programs and seminars. Some companies also provide special programs through colleges, universities, and outside agencies. Engineers usually advance from junior-level engineering positions to more senior-level positions through a series of positions. Engineers may also specialize in a specific area once they have acquired the necessary experience and skills.

Some engineers move into sales and managerial positions, with some engineers leaving the electronics industry to seek top-level management positions with other type of firms. Other engineers set up their own firms in design or consulting. Engineers can also move into the academic field and become teachers at high schools or universities.

The key to advancing in the electronics field is keeping pace with technological changes, which occur rapidly in this field. Electrical and electronics engineers will need to pursue additional training throughout their careers in order to stay up-to-date on new technologies and techniques.

Earnings

Starting salaries for all engineers are generally much higher than for workers in any other field. In 1999, entry-level electrical and electronics engineers with a bachelor's degree earned an average of $45,200, according to the National Association of Colleges and Employers. Electrical and electronics engineers with a master's degree averaged around $57,200 in their first jobs after graduation. The U.S. Department of Labor reports that the median annual salary for electrical and electronics engineers was $62,660 in 1998. Those who rise to the top of their fields can make more than $100,000 annually. The average annual salary for engineers who work for the government is around $68,000.

Most companies offer attractive benefits packages, although the actual benefits vary from company to company. Benefits can include any of the following: paid holidays, paid vacations, personal days, sick leave; medical, health, life insurance; short- and long-term disability insurance; profit sharing; 401(k) plans; retirement and pension plans; educational assistance; leave time for educational purposes; and credit unions. Some companies also offer computer purchase assistance plans and discounts on company products.

Work Environment

Tom's work hours are typically regular—9:00 to 5:00, Monday through Friday—although there is occasional overtime. In many parts of the country, this five-day, 40-hour work week is still the norm, but it is becoming much less common. Many engineers regularly work 10 or 20 hours of overtime a week. Engineers in research and development, or those conducting experiments, often need to work at night or on weekends. Workers who supervise production activities may need to come in during the evenings or on weekends to handle special production requirements. In addition to the time spent on the job, many engineers also participate in professional associations and pursue additional training during their free time. Many high-tech companies allow flex-time, which means that workers can arrange their own schedules within certain time frames.

Most electrical and electronics engineers work in fairly comfortable environments. Engineers involved in research and design may, like Tom, work in specially equipped laboratories. Engineers involved in development and manufacturing work in offices and may spend part of their time in production facilities. Depending on the type of work one does, there may be extensive travel. Engineers involved in field service and sales spend a significant time traveling to see clients. Engineers working for large corporations may travel to other plants and manufacturing companies, both around the country and at foreign locations.

Engineering professors spend part of their time teaching in classrooms, part of it doing research either in labs or libraries, and some of the time still connected with industry.

Outlook

More engineers work in the electrical and electronics field than in any other division of engineering. In the United States, there were approximately 357,000 such engineers holding jobs in the industry in 1998. Most worked in engineering and business consulting firms, manufacturing companies that produce electrical and electronic equipment, business machines, computers and data processing companies, and telecommunications parts. Others work for companies that make automotive electronics, scientific equipment, and aircraft parts; consulting firms; public utilities; and government agencies.

The demand for electrical and electronics engineers fluctuates with changes in the economy. In the late 1980s and early 1990s, many companies that produced defense products suffered from cutbacks in defense orders and, as a result, made reductions in their engineering staffs. However, opportunities in defense-related fields may improve, as there is a growing trend toward upgrading existing aircraft and weapons systems. In addition, the increased use of electronic components in automobiles and increases in computer and telecommunications production require a high number of skilled engineers. Opportunities for electrical and electronics engineers are expected to increase faster than the average for all other jobs through 2008, according to the *Occupational Outlook Handbook.*

The growing consumer, business, and government demand for improved computers and communications equipment is expected to propel much of this expected growth. Another area of high demand is projected to be the development of electrical and electronic goods for the consumer market. The strongest job growth, however, is likely to be in nonmanufacturing industries. This is because more and more firms are contracting for electronic engineering services from consulting and service firms.

Engineers will need to stay on top of changes within the electronics industry and will need additional training throughout their careers to learn new technologies. Economic trends and conditions within the global marketplace have become increasingly more important. In the past, most electronics production was done in the United States or by American-owned companies. During the 1990s, this changed, and the electronics industry entered an era of global production. Worldwide economies and production trends will have a larger impact on U.S. production, and companies that cannot compete technologically may not succeed. Job security is no longer a sure thing, and many engineers can expect to make significant changes in their careers at least once. Engineers who have a strong academic foundation, who have acquired technical knowledge and skills, and who stay up-to-date on changing technologies provide themselves with the versatility and flexibility to succeed within the electronics industry.

For More Information

For information on careers and educational programs, contact the following associations:
Institute of Electrical and Electronics Engineers
    1828 L Street, NW, Suite 1202
    Washington, DC 20036-5104
    Web: http://www.ieee.org/

Electronic Industries Alliance
2500 Wilson Boulevard
Arlington, VA 22201-3834
Tel: 703-907-7500
Web: http://www.eia.org

For information on careers, educational programs, and student clubs, contact:
Junior Engineering Technical Society, Inc.
1420 King Street, Suite 405
Alexandria, VA 22314-2794
Tel: 703-548-5387
Web: http://www.jets.org

For information on the Summer at Delphi Youth Program for high school students, contact:
The Delphian School
20950 SW Rock Creek Road
Sheridan, OR 97378
Tel: 800-626-6610
Email: info@delphian.org
Web: http://www.delphian.org

For information on its summer youth program for high school students, contact:
Michigan Technological University Summer Youth Program
Youth Programs Office
1400 Townsend Drive
Houghton, MI 49931-1295
Tel: 906-487-1885
Web: http://www.mtu.edu

Financial Services Brokers

Overview

Financial services brokers, *sometimes called* registered representatives, account executives, securities sales representatives, *or* stockbrokers, *work to represent both individuals and organizations who wish to invest in and sell stocks, bonds, or other financial products. Financial services brokers analyze companies offering stocks to see if investing in them is worth the risk. They also advise clients on proper investment strategies for their own investment goals.*

The Job

The most important part of a broker's job is finding customers and building a client base. Beginning brokers spend much of their time searching for customers, relying heavily on telephone solicitation "cold calls"—that is, calling people with whom they have never had any contact. They may also find customers through business and social contacts or be given a list of likely prospects from their brokerage firm.

When they open accounts for new customers, they first record all the personal information that is required to allow the customer to trade securities through the brokerage firm. Depending on a customer's knowledge of the market, the broker may explain the meaning of stock market terms and trading practices; offer financial counseling; and devise an individual financial portfolio for the customer, including securities, life insurance, corporate and municipal bonds, mutual funds, certificates of deposit, annuities, and other investments. The broker must determine the customer's investment goals—whether the customer wants long-term, steady growth or a quick turnaround of stocks for short-term gains—and then offers advice on investments accordingly. Once an investment strategy has been worked out, brokers execute buy and sell orders for their customers by relaying the information to the floor of the stock exchange, where the order is actually put into effect by a broker's floor representative. *Securities traders* also buy and sell securities, but usually as a representative of a private firm.

From the research department of the brokerage firm, brokers obtain information on the activities and projected growth of any company that is offering or will offer stock. The actual or perceived strength of a company is a major factor in a stock-purchase decision. Brokers must be prepared to answer questions on the technical aspects of stock market operations and also be informed on current economic conditions. They are expected to have the market knowledge to anticipate certain trends and to counsel customers accordingly in terms of their particular stock holdings.

Some financial services brokers specialize in specific areas such as handling only institutional accounts, bond issues, or mutual funds. Whatever their area of specialization, financial services brokers must keep abreast of all significant political and economic conditions, maintain very accurate records for all transactions, and continually solicit new customers.

Requirements

High School

If you are interested in becoming a financial services broker, you should take courses in business, accounting, economics, mathematics, government, and communications.

Postsecondary Training

Because of the specialized knowledge necessary to perform this job properly, a college education is increasingly important, especially in the larger brokerage houses. To make intelligent and insightful judgments, a broker must be able to read and understand financial reports and evaluate statistics. For this reason, although employers seldom require specialized academic training, a bachelor's degree in business administration, economics, or finance is helpful.

Certification or Licensing

Almost all states require brokers to be licensed. Some states administer written examinations and some require brokers to post a personal bond. Beginning brokers must register as representatives of their firms in accordance with the regulations set forth by the securities exchange where they do business or the National Association of Securities Dealers (NASD). In order to qualify as registered representatives, brokers must first pass the General Securities Registered Representative Examination, administered by the NASD. Many states require brokers to take and pass a second examination—the Uniform Securities Agents State Law Examination.

Other Requirements

Because they deal with the public, brokers should be well groomed and pleasant and have large reserves of tact and patience. Employers look for ambitious individuals with sales ability. Brokers also need self-confidence and the ability to handle frequent rejections. Above all, they must have a highly developed sense of responsibility, because in many instances they will be handling funds that represent a client's life savings.

Exploring

Any sales experience can provide you with a general background for work in financial services. Occasionally, young people can find summer employment in a brokerage house. A visit to a local investment office, the New York Stock Exchange, or one of the commodities exchanges located in other major cities will provide a valuable opportunity to observe how transactions are handled and what is required of people in the field.

Employers

Financial services brokers work in brokerage and investment firms all around the country. Although many of these firms are very small, the largest employers of financial services brokers are a few large firms that have their main offices in major cities, especially New York.

Starting Out

Many firms hire beginning workers in sales, train them, and then retain them for a probationary period to determine their talents and ability to succeed in the business. The training period lasts about six months and includes classroom instruction and on-the-job training. Applications for these beginning jobs may be made directly to the personnel offices of the various securities firms. Check your local Yellow Pages or the Internet for listings of securities firms.

Advancement

Depending upon their skills and ambitions, financial services brokers may advance rapidly in this field. Accomplished brokers may find that the size and number of accounts they service will increase to a point at which they no longer need to solicit new customers. Others become branch managers, research analysts, or partners in their own firms.

Earnings

The salaries of trainees and beginners range from $1,200 to $1,500 per month, although larger firms pay a somewhat higher starting wage. Once the financial services broker has acquired a sufficient number of accounts, he or she works solely on a commission basis, with fees resulting from the size and type of security bought or sold. Some firms pay annual bonuses to their brokers when business warrants. Since earnings can fluctuate greatly based on the condition of the market, some brokers may find it necessary to supplement their income through other means during times of slow market activity.

According to the U.S. Department of Labor, the median earnings for brokers were $48,090 a year in 1998; the middle 50 percent earned between $31,400 and $103,040. Ten percent earned less than $22,660 and 10 percent earned more than $124,800.

Work Environment

Brokers work more flexible hours than workers in other fields. They may work fewer hours during dull trading periods but be required to put in overtime dealing with paperwork during busy periods.

The atmosphere of a brokerage firm is frequently highly charged, and the peaks and drops of market activity can produce a great deal of tension. Watching fortunes being made is exciting, but the reverse occurs frequently, too, and it requires responsibility and maturity to weather the setbacks.

Outlook

The U.S. Department of Labor predicts that job opportunities for financial services brokers are expected to grow much faster than the average for all occupations through the year 2008 because of continued interest in the stock market. The strong growth of the economy, rising personal incomes, and greater inherited wealth are increasing the amount of funds people are able to invest. Many people dabble in investing via their personal computers and the Internet. Even those with limited means have the option of investing through a variety of methods such as investment clubs, mutual funds, and monthly payment plans. In addition, the expansion of business activities and new technological breakthroughs will create increased demand for the sale of stock to meet capital requirements for companies around the world.

Demand for financial services brokers fluctuates with the economy. Turnover among beginners is high because they have a hard time soliciting enough clients. Because of potentially high earnings, competition in this business is very intense.

For More Information

For information on the General Securities Registered Representative Examination and to obtain a free publication about how to become a financial services broker, contact:

National Association of Securities Dealers
9513 Key West Avenue
Rockville, MD 20850-3389
Tel: 301-590-6500
Web: http://www.nasd.com

For information on the securities industry, contact:

The Securities Industry Association
120 Broadway, 35th Floor
New York, NY 10271-0080
Tel: 212-608-1500
Web: http://www.sia.com

Graphic Designers

Graphic designers are practical artists whose creations are intended to express ideas, convey information, or draw attention to a product. They design a wide variety of materials including advertisements, displays, packaging, signs, computer graphics and games, book and magazine covers and interiors, animated characters, and company logos to fit the needs and preferences of their various clients.

The Job

Graphic designers are not primarily fine artists, although they may be highly skilled at drawing or painting. Most designs commissioned to graphic designers involve both artwork and copy (that is, words). Thus, the designer must not only be familiar with the wide range of art media (photography, drawing, painting, collage, etc.) and styles, but he or she must also be familiar with a wide range of typefaces and know how to manipulate them for the right effect. Because design tends to change in a similar way to fashion, designers must keep up to date with the latest trends. At the same time, they must be well grounded in more traditional, classic designs.

Graphic designers can work as in-house designers for a particular company, as staff designers for a graphic design firm, or as freelance designers working for themselves. Some designers specialize in designing advertising materials or packaging. Others focus on corporate identity materials such as company stationery and logos. Some work mainly for publishers designing book and magazine covers and page layouts. Some work in the area of computer graphics, creating still or animated graphics for computer software, videos, or motion pictures. A highly specialized type of graphic designer, the environmental graphic designer, designs large outdoor signs. Some graphic designers design exclusively on the computer, while others may use both the computer and traditional hand drawings or paintings, depending on the project's needs and requirements.

Whatever the specialty and whatever their medium, all graphic designers take a similar approach to a project, whether it is for an entirely new design or for a variation on an existing one. Graphic designers begin by determining as best they can the needs and preferences of the clients and the potential users, buyers, or viewers.

In the case of a graphic designer working on a company logo, for example, he or she will likely meet with company representatives to discuss such points as how and where the company is going to use the logo and what size, color, and shape preferences company executives might have. Project budgets must be carefully respected: a design that may be perfect in every way but that is too costly to reproduce is basically useless. Graphic designers may need to compare their ideas with similar ones from other companies and analyze the image they project. Thus they must have a good knowledge of how various colors, shapes, and layouts affect the viewer psychologically.

After a plan has been conceived and the details worked out, the graphic designer does some preliminary designs (generally two or three) to present to the client for approval. The client may reject the preliminary design entirely and request a new design, or he or she may ask the designer to make alterations to the existing design. The designer then goes back to the drawing board to attempt a new design or make the requested changes. This process continues until the client approves the design.

Once a design has been approved, the graphic designer prepares the design for professional reproduction, that is, printing. The printer may require a "mechanical," in which the artwork and copy are arranged on a white board just as it is to be photographed, or the designer may be asked to submit an electronic copy of the design. Either way, designers must have a good understanding of the printing process, including color separation, paper properties, and halftone (i.e., photograph) reproduction.

Requirements

High School

High school students should take any art and design courses that are available. Computer classes are also helpful, particularly those that teach page layout programs or art and photography manipulation programs. Working on the school newspaper or yearbook can provide valuable design experience. You may also volunteer to design flyers or posters for school events.

Postsecondary Training

More graphic designers are recognizing the value of formal training, and at least two out of three people entering the field today have a college degree or some college education. Over one hundred colleges and art schools offer graphic design programs that are accredited by the National Association of Schools of Art and Design. At many schools, graphic design students must take a year of basic art and design courses before being accepted into the bachelor's degree program. In addition, applicants to the bachelor's degree programs in graphic arts may be asked to submit samples of their work to prove artistic ability. Many schools and employers depend on samples, or portfolios, to evaluate the applicants' skills in graphic design.

Many programs increasingly emphasize the importance of using computers for design work. Computer proficiency among graphic designers will be very important in the years to come. Interested individuals should select an academic program that incorporates computer training into the curriculum, or train themselves on their own.

A bachelor of fine arts program at a four-year college or university may include courses such as principles of design, art and art history, painting, sculpture, mechanical and architectural drawing, architecture, computerized design, basic engineering, fashion designing and sketching, garment construction, and textiles. Such degrees are desirable but not always necessary for obtaining a position as a graphic designer.

Other Requirements

As with all artists, graphic designers need a degree of artistic talent, creativity, and imagination. They must be sensitive to beauty and have an eye for detail and a strong sense of color, balance, and proportion. To a great extent, these qualities are natural, but they can be developed through training, both on the job and in professional schools, colleges, and universities.

More and more graphic designers need solid computer skills and working knowledge of several of the common drawing, image editing, and page layout programs. Graphic design on the computer is done on both Macintosh systems and on PC systems; many designers have both types of computers in their studios.

With or without specialized education, graphic designers seeking employment should have a good portfolio containing samples of their best work. The graphic designer's portfolio is extremely important and can make a difference when an employer must choose between two otherwise equally qualified candidates.

A period of on-the-job training is expected for all beginning designers. The length of time it takes to become fully qualified as a graphic designer may run from one to three years, depending on prior education and experience as well as innate talent.

Exploring

High school students interested in a career in graphic design have a number of ways to find out whether they have the talent, ambition, and perseverance to succeed in the field. Students should take as many art and design courses as possible while still in high school and should become proficient at working on computers. In addition, to get an insider's view of various design occupations, they could enlist the help of art teachers or school guidance counselors to make arrangements to tour design companies and interview designers.

While studying, students interested in graphic design can get practical experience by participating in school and community projects that call for design talents. These might include such activities as building sets for plays, setting up exhibits, planning seasonal and holiday displays, and preparing programs and other printed materials. For those interested in publication design, work on the school newspaper or yearbook is invaluable.

Part-time and summer jobs offer would-be designers an excellent way to become familiar with the day-to-day requirements of a particular design occupation and gain some basic related experience. Possible places of employment include design studios, design departments in advertising agencies and manufacturing companies, department and furniture stores, flower shops, workshops that produce ornamental items, and museums. Museums also use a number of volunteer workers. Inexperienced people are often employed as sales, clerical, or general helpers; those with a little more education and experience may qualify for jobs in which they have a chance to develop actual design skills and build portfolios of completed design projects.

Employers

Graphic designers work in many different industries, including the wholesale and retail trade (department stores, furniture and home furnishings stores, apparel stores, florist shops); manufacturing industries (machinery, motor vehicles and aircraft, metal products, instruments, apparel, textiles, printing and publishing); service industries (business services, engineering, architecture); construction firms; and government agencies. Public relations and publicity firms, advertising agencies, commercial printers, and mail-order houses all have graphic design departments. The publishing industry is a primary employer of graphic designers, including book publishers, magazines, newspapers, and newsletters. Many graphic designers are self-employed, and hire their freelance services to multiple clients.

Starting Out

The best way to enter the field of graphic design is to have a strong portfolio. Potential employers rely on portfolios to evaluate talent and how that talent might be used to fit the company's special needs. Beginning graphic designers can assemble a portfolio from work completed at school, in art classes, and in part-time or freelance jobs. The portfolio should continually be updated to reflect the designer's growing skills, so it will always be ready for possible job changes.

Job interviews may be obtained by applying directly to companies that employ designers. Many colleges and professional schools have placement services to help their graduates find positions, and sometimes it is possible to get a referral from a previous part-time employer or volunteer coordinator.

Advancement

As part of their on-the-job training, beginning graphic designers generally are given the simpler tasks and work under direct supervision. As they gain experience, they move up to more complex work with increasingly less supervision.

Experienced graphic designers, especially those with leadership capabilities, may be promoted to chief designer, design department head, or other supervisory positions.

Computer graphic designers can move into other computer-related positions with additional education. Some may become interested in graphics programming in order to further improve computer design capabilities. Others may want to become involved with multimedia and interactive graphics. Video games, touch-screen displays in stores, and even laser light shows are all products of multimedia graphic designers.

When designers develop personal styles that are in high demand in the marketplace, they sometimes go into business for themselves. Freelance design work can be erratic, however, so usually only the most experienced designers with an established client base can count on consistent full-time work.

Earnings

The range of salaries for graphic designers is quite broad. Many earn as little as $17,000, while others receive more than $35,000. Salaries depend primarily on the nature and scope of the employer, with computer graphic designers earning wages on the high end of the range.

Self-employed designers can earn a lot one year and substantially more or less the next. Their earnings depend on individual talent and business ability, but, in general, are higher than those of salaried designers, although like any self-employed individual, they must pay their own insurance costs and taxes and are not compensated for vacation or sick days.

The Society of Publication Designers has estimated that entry-level graphic designers earned between $23,000 and $27,000 annually in 1997. Salaried designers who advance to the position of design manager or design director earn about $60,000 a year and, at the level of corporate vice-president, make $70,000 and up. The owner of a consulting firm can make $85,000 or more.

Graphic designers who work for large corporations receive full benefits, including health insurance, paid vacation, and sick leave.

Work Environment

Most graphic designers work regular hours in clean, comfortable, pleasant offices or studios. Conditions vary depending on the design specialty.

Some graphic designers work in small establishments with few employees; others, in large organizations with large design departments. Some deal mostly with their co-workers; others may have a lot of public contact. Freelance designers are paid by the assignment. To maintain a steady income, they must constantly strive to please their clients and to find new ones.

Computer graphic designers may have to work long, irregular hours in order to complete an especially ambitious project.

Outlook

Chances for employment look very good for qualified graphic designers through the year 2008, especially for those involved with computer graphics. The design field in general is expected to grow at a faster than average rate. As computer graphic technology continues to advance, there will be a need for well-trained computer graphic designers. Companies that have always used graphics will expect their designers to perform work on computers. Companies for which graphic design was once too time consuming or costly are now sprucing up company newsletters and magazines, among other things, and need graphic designers to do it.

Because the design field is a popular one, appealing to many talented individuals, competition is expected to be strong in all areas. Beginners and designers with only average talent or without formal education and technical skills may encounter some difficulty in securing employment.

About one-third of all graphic designers are self-employed, a higher proportion than is found in most other occupations.

For More Information

For more information about careers in graphic design, contact the following organizations:

American Center for Design
325 West Huron, Suite 711
Chicago, IL 60610
Tel: 312-787-2018
Web: http://www.ac4d.org/

American Institute of Graphic Arts
164 Fifth Avenue
New York, NY 10160-1652
Tel: 800-548-1634
Email: aiganatl@aol.com
Web: http://www.aiga.org

National Association of Schools of Art and Design
11250 Roger Bacon Drive, Suite 21
Reston, VA 22090
Tel: 703-437-0700
Email: info@arts-accredit.org
Web: http://www.arts-accredit.org/nasad/default.htm

Society for Environmental Graphic Design
401 F Street, NW, Suite 333
Washington, DC 20001
Tel: 202-638-5555
Email: SEGDOFFICE@aol.com
Web: http://www.segd.org/

Society of Publication Designers
60 East 42nd Street, Suite 721
New York, NY 10165
Tel: 212-983-8585
Web: http://www.spd.org/

Hardware Engineers

Overview

Computer hardware engineers *design, build, and test computer hardware—computer chips, circuit boards— as well as computer systems and software. They may also work with peripheral devices such as printers, scanners, modems, and monitors, among others. Hardware engineers are employed by a variety of companies, some of which specialize in business, accounting, science, or engineering. Most hardware engineers have a degree in computer science or engineering or equivalent computer background.*

The Job

Calvin Prior is a network systems administrator for TASC, a nonprofit social service agency headquartered in Chicago, Illinois. He is responsible for the day-to-day operations of a state-wide network of 300+ servers. Calvin starts work early; most mornings he's at his desk by 7:30 AM. His first task of the day is making sure the network files from the previous day backed up successfully. Then he checks for email and voice mail messages and promptly responds to urgent problems.

Daily meetings are held to keep informed on department business. "It's very short and informal," says Calvin. "We discuss urgent business or upcoming projects and schedules." The rest of the morning is spent working on various projects, troubleshooting systems, or phone work with TASC's remote offices. After a quick lunch break and if no network breakdowns or glitches occur, Calvin usually spends his afternoons researching hardware products or responding to user requests.

The workload changes daily, leaving some days more hectic than others. "It's important to be flexible," says Calvin. "And be good at multi-tasking." If a major problem cannot be solved over the phone, Calvin must travel to the source. Solutions are not always simple; some require changing hardware or redesigning the system. Calvin often upgrades or reworks systems in the early morning, late at night, or on weekends to minimize the disruption of work. Major network problems require a complete shutdown of the entire system. "The less number of servers on the network, the better," he says.

Engineering professionals like Calvin must be familiar with different network systems such as Local Area Networks (LAN), Wide Area Networks (WAN), among others, as well as programming languages suited to their company's needs. Many work as part of a team of specialists who use elements of science, math, and electronics to improve existing technology or implement solutions.

Requirements

High School

Calvin credits high school computer and electronic classes and programming courses as giving him a head start in this career. You should also take speech and writing courses so that you will be able to communicate effectively with co-workers and clients.

Postsecondary Training

Calvin initially studied electrical engineering at the University of Illinois, Champaign-Urbana, but transferred and eventually graduated with an associate's degree in electronics from Parkland Community College. The hands-on approach at Parkland appealed to Calvin. "Most of our classes were held in the late afternoon and evening because many of the instructors held real computer industry jobs in addition to their teaching duties."

Certification or Licensing

Not all computer professionals are certified—the deciding factor seems to be if it is required by their employer. Many companies offer tuition reimbursement, or incentives, to those who earn certification. Certification is available in a variety of specialties. The Institute for Certification of Computing Professionals (ICCP), for example, offers the designation Certified Computing Professional, after successful completion of required study and examination. Certification is held by many as a measure of industry knowledge as well as leverage when negotiating salary.

Other Requirements

What do companies look for in new hires? Industry insiders say patience, self-motivation, and a broad range of computer skills. Flexibility is another important skill. Often, a number of projects are worked on simultaneously, so according to Calvin, "multi-tasking is important."

Employers

Computer hardware engineers are employed in nearly every industry by small and large corporations alike. According to the *Occupational Outlook Quarterly,* the majority of hardware engineers are employed by the computer and data processing and electronics manufacturing industries.

Jobs are plentiful nationwide, though salary averages, as reported by a recent *Computerworld* survey, tend to be higher in New York City and Los Angeles. Note however that these cities are notorious for their high cost of living, which, in the end, may offset a higher income.

Starting Out

Education and solid work experience will open industry doors. Though a bachelor's degree is a minimum requirement for most corporate giants, some companies, smaller ones especially, will hire based largely on work experience and practical training. Many computer professionals employed in the computer industry for some time do not have traditional electrical engineering or computer science degrees, but rather moved up on the basis of their work record. However, if you aspire to a management position, or want to work as a teacher, then having a college degree is a necessity.

Large computer companies aggressively recruit on campus armed with signing bonuses and other incentives. Employment opportunities are posted in newspaper want ads daily, with some papers devoting a separate section to computer-related positions. The Internet offers a wealth of employment information plus several sites for browsing job openings, or to post your resume. Most companies maintain a Web page where they post employment opportunities or solicit resumes.

Like other fields in the computer industry, demand for computer engineers is so great, schools can't seem to supply enough graduates. Calvin agrees. "There is a lack of quality workers," he says. "One of our biggest problems is being understaffed."

Advancement

Many companies hire new grads to work as junior engineers. Problem solving skills and the ability to implement solutions is a big part of this entry-level job. With enough work experience, junior engineers can move into positions that focus on a particular area in the computer industry, say networks or peripherals. Landing a senior level engineering position, systems architect for example, is possible after considerable work experience and study. Aspiring hardware engineers should hone their computer skills to the highest level—that means keeping abreast of the latest technology with continuing education, certification, or even advanced computer study. Many high-level engineers hold a master's degree or better.

Some computer professionals working on the technical side of the industry opt to switch over to the marketing side of the business. Advancement opportunities here may include positions in product management or sales.

Earnings

According to a 1998 National Association of Colleges and Employers salary survey, hardware design and development engineers with a bachelor's degree in computer science earn an average starting salary of $43,312. In comparison, graduates with an engineering background earn an average annual salary between $35,705 and $40,750. Graduates of master's programs in computer engineering have average starting salaries of about $50,650; starting salaries for holders of doctorates are even higher.

The demand for talented and educated workers is very strong, causing many companies to offer incentives or signing bonuses to lure prospective employees. Other job perks, besides the usual benefit package—insurance, vacation, sick time, profit sharing—may include stock options, continuing education or training, tuition reimbursement, flexible hours, and child care or other on-site services.

Work Environment

Most hardware engineers work 40- to 50-hour weeks or more depending on the project to which they are assigned. Weekend work is common with some positions. Contrary to popular perceptions, hardware engineers do not spend their workdays cooped up in their offices. Instead, they spend the majority of their time meeting, planning, and working with various staff members from different levels of management and technical expertise. Since it takes numerous workers to take a project from start to finish, team players are in high demand.

Outlook

Computer engineering will be one of the three fastest growing occupations through the year 2008, according to the *Occupational Outlook Handbook*. Industry growth can be attributed to factors such as greater business use of the Internet; the networking of information and resources within a company; and technical advancements. Investment in a college education—good major choices are engineering, Management Information Systems (MIS), or computer science, or solid computer-related courses, such as computer systems analysis, computer programming, among others—will help you secure a promising employment future. Also, don't forget the value of on-the-job training and work experience with networks, databases, and other systems.

In addition to new job opportunities, many positions will open as a result of current computer professionals leaving the industry due to retirement or other reasons.

For More Information

For information regarding the computer industry, career opportunities as a computer engineer, or the association's membership requirements, contact:
Association for Computing Machinery
One Astor Plaza
1515 Broadway
New York, NY 10036
Tel: 800-342-6626
Email: ACMHELP@acm.org
Web: http://www.acm.org
and http://www.acm.org/membership/student/

For certification information, contact:
Institute for Certification of Computing Professionals
2200 East Devon Avenue, Suite 247
Des Plaines, IL 60018-4503
Tel: 847-299-4227
Web: http://www.iccp.org

For information on a career in computer engineering, computer scholarships, or a copy of Computer Magazine, *contact:*
IEEE Computer Society
1730 Massachusetts Avenue, NW
Washington, DC 20036-1992
Tel: 202-371-0101
Web: http://www.computer.org

For employment information, links to online career sites for computer professionals, and background on the industry, contact:
Institute of Electrical and Electronics Engineers
3 Park Avenue, 17th Floor
New York, NY 10016-5997
Web: http://www.ieee.org

Health Care Managers

Health care managers, *also known as* health services managers *and* health services administrators, *direct the operation of hospitals, nursing homes, and other health care organizations. They are responsible for facilities, services, programs, staff, budgets, and relations with other organizations.*

The Job

Health care managers, or chief executive officers (CEOs) of hospitals and health care facilities, organize and manage personnel, equipment, and auxiliary services. They are responsible for hiring and supervising personnel, handling budgets and the fee schedule to be charged patients, and establishing billing procedures. In addition, they help plan space needs, purchase supplies and equipment, oversee building and equipment maintenance, and provide for mail, phones, laundry, and other services for patients and staff. In some health care institutions, many of these duties are delegated to assistants or to various department heads. These assistants may supervise operations in such clinical areas as surgery, nursing, dietary, or therapy and in such administrative areas as purchasing, finance, housekeeping, and maintenance.

The health services administrator works closely with the institution's governing board in the development of plans and policies. Following the board's directions, the administrator may carry out large projects that expand and develop hospital services. Such projects include organizing fund-raising campaigns and planning new research projects.

Health services managers meet regularly with their staffs to discuss achievements and solve the facility's problems. Managers may organize training programs for nurses, interns, and others in cooperation with the medical staff and department heads. Health care executives also represent the health care facility at community or professional meetings.

Requirements

High School

If you are interested in a health managerial career, you should start preparing in high school by taking college preparatory classes. Because communication is important, take as many speech and writing classes as possible. Courses in health, business, mathematics, business, and computer science are also excellent choices to help you prepare for this career.

Postsecondary Training

The training required to qualify for this work depends, to a large extent, on the qualifications established by the individual employer or a facility's governing board. Most prefer people with a graduate degree in health services administration. A few require that their chief executives be physicians, while others look for people with formal training in law or general business administration as well as experience in the health care field. The future health care administrator may have a liberal arts foundation with a strong background in the social sciences or business economics.

Specialized training in health services administration is offered at both graduate and undergraduate levels. The graduate program is generally a two-year course spent in academic work and with additional months spent as an administrative resident, a full-time on-the-job training post in a facility approved by the university the candidate attends. Successful completion of the course work, the residency, and perhaps a thesis is required to earn the master's degree. An optional third-year fellowship provides additional work experience supervised by a mentor. During this period, the individual may work in various hospital departments as an assistant to department heads.

Certification or Licensing

Licensure is not a requirement for health care services executives employed in short-term, general hospitals. However, all states require nursing home administrators to be licensed. Since requirements vary from state to state, those considering careers in nursing home administration should contact the state licensing body for licensure requirements. Also, it should be noted that continuing education is now a condition of licensure in most states.

Other Requirements

Much of the work consists of dealing with people—the hospital's governing board, the medical staff, the department heads and other employees, the patients and their families, and community leaders and businesses. Therefore health services managers must be tactful and sympathetic.

Administrators must, in addition, be able to coordinate the facility's many related functions. They need to understand, for instance, financial operations, purchasing, organizational development, and public relations. They must also have the ability to make some decisions with speed and others with considerable study. And, of course, health services executives should have a deep interest in health care and the problems of sick and injured patients.

Special hospitals, such as mental hospitals, often employ administrators who are physicians in the facility's specialty. Usually, facilities which are operated by religious groups employ administrators of the same faith as those of the group operating the hospital.

Exploring

Young people considering a career as a health services manager should take advantage of opportunities in high school to develop some of the skills required in this occupation. Since administrators and other health care executives should be leaders and talented speakers, participation in clubs as a leader or active member and in debate and speech clubs is helpful. Working in the school's health center is also useful. Hospitals, nursing homes, and other health service facilities offer part-time work after school, on weekends, and during the summer. Health services executives are often willing to speak to interested students, but it is suggested that students make an appointment first.

Courses in business law, psychology, and other social sciences, as well as computer science, can also help in evaluating interest in hospital or health services administration.

Employers

Health care managers can find employment in facilities such as HMOs and group medical practices, surgicenters and centers for urgent care, cardiac rehabilitation, diagnostic imaging, and so forth. Opportunities are also plentiful in long-term care facilities, such as nursing homes, home health care agencies, adult day care programs, life care communities, and other residential facilities.

Starting Out

A student in training as an administrative resident or postgraduate fellow may be offered a job as an administrative assistant or a department head by the hospital or health care facility where the residency is served. The hospital's administrator at the place of training also may assist the student in locating a job.

Notice of job openings can often be found by contacting the university's placement bureau or through bulletins of state and national associations. Large professional society meetings may offer on-site notices of job openings; interviews can often be arranged on site. Positions in federal- and state-operated health care institutions are filled by the civil service or by political appointment. Appointments to armed forces hospitals are handled by the various branches of the services.

Although the four-year college program followed by graduate work is becoming the accepted method of entry, it is still possible to gain experience and training in subordinate positions and work up the administrative ladder.

Advancement

It is unusual to finish college and step into a position as an upper-level health services executive. People usually must gain experience that qualifies them for advancement by working in more specialized clinical or administrative areas found in a health care facility. Experience obtained in administration of health care personnel, information systems, budget, patient care, and finance is valuable. Experience and graduate work often leads to promotion as a department head in one of these administrative areas. Those with graduate training can expect to achieve higher-level positions. Assistant administrator or vice president is often the next step and may lead to appointment as the hospital's chief executive.

Earnings

Salaries of health services executives depend on the type of facility, geographic location, the size of the administrative staff, the budget, and the policy of the governing board. The *Occupational Outlook Handbook* reports that the median annual earnings for health care managers was $48,870 in 1998. The lowest 10 percent earned less than $28,600 a year, while the highest 10 percent earned more than $88,730. A 1998 survey conducted by *Modern Healthcare* reported that median annual salaries varied by clinical department. Managers in respiratory therapy earned $57,700; ambulatory/outpatient services, $66,200; radiology, $66,800; physical therapy, $68,100; rehabilitation services, $73,400; and nursing services, $100,200.

According to the Buck Survey conducted by the American Health Care Association, nursing home administrators earned a median salary of

$52,800 in 1997. Fifty percent earned between $44,300 to $60,300 annually. Assistant nursing home administrators earned a median salary of about $35,000 a year.

Health service administrators managing a small group practice, consisting of seven or fewer physicians, averaged $60,000 annually in 1998, as reported by the Medical Group Management Association. Administrators responsible for practices with more than seven physicians earned an average of $76,700.

Some administrators receive free meals, housing, and laundry service, depending on the facility in which they are employed. They usually receive paid vacations and holidays, sick leave, hospitalization and insurance benefits, and pension programs. The executive benefits package nowadays often includes management incentive bonuses based on job performance ranging from $25,700 to $225,000.

Work Environment

To perform efficiently as an executive, health services administrators usually work out of a large office. They must maintain good communication with the staff and members of various departments.

Most administrators work five and one half days each week, averaging about 55 to 60 hours, but hours can be irregular since hospitals and other health care facilities operate around the clock, and emergencies may require the manager's supervision any time of the day or night.

Outlook

Since every hospital and numerous other health care facilities employ administrators, employment opportunities in health care will be excellent through the year 2008 as the industry continues to diversify and deal with the problems of financing health care for everyone. The U.S. Department of Labor predicts that employment will grow at a rate faster than the average. Not all areas will grow at the same rate, however. Changes in the health care system are taking place because of the need to control escalating costs. This will have the greatest impact on hospitals, traditionally the largest employer of health services executives. The number of hospitals is declining as separate companies are set up to provide services such as ambulatory surgery, alcohol and drug rehabilitation, or home health care. So, while hospitals themselves may offer fewer jobs, many new openings are expected to be available in other health care settings. Colleges and universities are graduating more health services managers than hospitals and other health care facilities can employ. As a result, competition for administrative jobs will be stiff. However, many starting executives can find jobs working in health care settings other than hospitals, or they may be offered jobs at the department head or staff levels.

With hospitals adopting a more business-like approach aimed at lowering costs and increasing earnings, demand for MBA graduates should remain steady. Those with strong people skills, as well as business or management skills, will find excellent opportunities as administrators in nursing homes and other long-term facilities, where a graduate degree in health services administration is increasingly required.

For More Information

American College of Health Care Administrators
1800 Diagonal Road, Suite 355
Alexandria, VA 22314
Tel: 703-739-7900
Email: info@achca.org
Web: http://www.achca.org/

Visit the ACHE Web site for information on accredited educational institutions and to read the online pamphlet, Your Career as a Healthcare Executive.
American College of Healthcare Executives (ACHE)
One North Franklin Street, Suite 1700
Chicago, IL 60606-3491
Tel: 312-424-2800
Web: http://www.ache.org

For information on health care administration careers, scholarships, and accredited programs, contact:
Association of University Programs in Health Administration
730 11th Street, NW, 4th Floor
Washington, DC 20001-4510
Tel: 202-638-1448
Web: http://www.aupha.org/

National Health Council
1730 M Street, NW, Suite 500
Washington, DC 20036
Tel: 202-785-3910
Email: info@nhcouncil.org
Web: http://www.nhcouncil.org/

Illustrators

Overview

Illustrators *prepare drawings for advertisements, magazines, books, newspapers, advertising, packaging, Web sites, computer programs, and other formats.* Medical illustrators *have special training in biology and the physical sciences. They use this training to draw accurate illustrations of parts of the human body or animals and plants.* Fashion illustrators *specialize in distinctive illustrations of the latest women's and men's fashions.*

The Job

Illustrators create artwork for both commercial and fine art purposes. They use a variety of media—pencil, pen and ink, pastels, paints (oil, acrylic, watercolor), airbrush, collage, and computer technology. Illustrations are used to decorate, describe, inform, clarify, instruct, and draw attention. They appear everywhere in print and electronic formats, including books, magazines, newspapers, signs and billboards, packaging (everything from milk cartons to CDs), Web sites, computer programs, greeting cards, calendars, stationery, and direct mail.

Illustrators often work as part of a creative team which includes graphic designers, photographers, and those who draw lettering, or *calligraphers.*

Illustrators work in almost every industry. Medical illustration and fashion illustration are two of the fastest growing specialties.

Medical illustrators open the visual world of the medical field through graphics, drawings, and photographs that make things easier to understand. Medical illustrators provide illustrations of anatomical and biological structures and processes, as well as surgical and medical techniques and procedures.

Medical illustrators work in a specialized area of technical illustration. These illustrators are concerned with representing human anatomy and processes, as well as other biological information. Their work is found in medical textbooks, magazines and journals, advertisements for medical products, instructional films and videotapes, television programs, exhibits, lectures and presentations, and computer-assisted learning programs. Some medical illustrators create three-dimensional physical models, such as anatomical teaching models, models used for teaching medical procedures, and also prosthetics.

The role of the medical illustrator is to aid in making medical and biological information, procedures, and techniques more understandable. They combine a knowledge of biology and anatomy with strong artistic and graphic skills.

Medical illustrators generally work with physicians, surgeons, biologists, and other scientists. When detailing a surgical procedure, they may observe the surgeon during surgery, and take instruction and advice from the surgeon about which parts of an operation to illustrate. They may illustrate parts of the body: the eye, the skeletal structure, the muscular structure, the structure of a cell, etc., for textbooks, encyclopedias, medical product brochures, and related literature. They may work with researchers to identify new organisms, develop new drugs, and examine cell structures, illustrating aspects of the researchers' work. They may also assist in developing sophisticated computer simulations, which allow physicians in training to "perform" a surgical procedure entirely on a computer before they are skilled enough to operate on actual patients. Medical illustrators also animate physical, biological, and anatomical processes for films and videotapes. Some medical illustrators sculpt or build three-dimensional models as well.

A medical illustrator may work in a wide range of medical and biological areas or specialize in a particular area, such as cell structure, blood, disease, or the eye. Much of their work is done with computers; however, they must still have strong skills in traditional drawing and drafting techniques.

Fashion illustrators work in a glamorized, intense environment. Their artistic focus is specifically on styles of clothing and personal image. Illustrators can work in a few different categories of the fashion field. They provide artwork to accompany editorial pieces in magazines such as *Glamour, Redbook,* and *Seventeen* and newspapers such as *Women's Wear Daily.* Catalog companies employ fashion illustrators to provide the artwork that sells their merchandise.

Fashion illustrators also work with fashion designers, editors, and models. They make sketches from designers' notes or they may sketch live models during runway shows or other fashion presentations. They may use pencils, pen and ink, charcoal, paint, or a combination of media. Fashion illustrators may work as freelancers, handling all the business aspects that go along with being self-employed.

Requirements

High School

Creative talent is more important in this field than education. This is a career field in which you aren't really required to pass certain classes in high school and college. However, there are academic programs in illustration at most colleges and universities and many adult education centers. Some high schools also offer elective classes in art and photography.

Postsecondary Training

To find a salaried position as an general illustrator, you will need at least a high school diploma and preferably an associate's degree in commercial art or fine art. The *Occupational Outlook Handbook* says 9 out of 10 visual artists have a college degree. Whether you are looking for a full-time employment or freelance assignments, you will need a portfolio that contains samples of your best work. Employers are especially interested in work that has been published or printed.

An advantage to pursuing education beyond high school is that it gives you an opportunity to build your portfolio—a collection of the best of your sketches, including work that shows prospective clients a variety of your skills. In addition to studying art, it is advantageous to study clothing construction, fashion design, or cosmetology.

Medical illustrators are required to complete an advanced degree program in medical illustration. You may enter graduate school with a bachelor's degree in either art or biology. Medical illustration programs usually include training in traditional illustration and design techniques, computer illustration, two-dimensional and three-dimensional animation, prosthetics, medical computer graphics, instructional design and technology, photography, motion media production, and pharmaceutical advertising. Coursework will also include pharmacology, basic sciences including anatomy and physiology, pathology, histology, embryology, neuroanatomy, and surgical observation and/or participation.

After college, you must attend one of the six accredited graduate programs in medical illustration. These programs last from two to three years and are offered at five U.S. institutions and one in Canada. These programs are accredited by the Committee on Allied Health Education and Accreditation (CAHEA) of the American Medical Association.

Fashion illustrators need to understand garment construction and fabrics. Reading fashion magazines will help you understand fashion trends as well as trends in illustration. You may be able to find work as a retail clerk in a clothing store to give you exposure to the fashion world.

Certification or Licensing

Illustrators need to continue their education and training while pursuing their careers. Licensing is not required in this field. While certification is not mandatory, you must keep up with the latest innovations in design techniques, computer software, and presentation technology, as well as technological advances in the fields for which you provide illustrations.

Most medical illustrators are members of the Association of Medical Illustrators (AMI). The AMI works with the CAHEA to establish accreditation and curriculum standards, offer certification in medical illustration, and provide other educational and support services to members and prospective members of this profession.

Other Requirements

Illustrators must be creative, and, of course, demonstrate artistic talent and skill. They also need to be flexible. Because their art is often commercial in nature, illustrators must be willing to accommodate their employers' desires if they are to build a broad clientele and earn a decent living. They must be able to take suggestions and rejections gracefully.

Exploring

You can explore an interest in this career by taking art courses. Participation in art, science, and fashion clubs is good exposure. Artists can always improve their drawing skills by practicing on their own, either producing original artwork, or making sketches from drawings that appear in textbooks and reference manuals that relate to their interests.

Employers

Six out of 10 visual artists are self-employed. Illustrators who are not self-employed work in advertising agencies, design firms, commercial art and reproduction firms, or printing and publishing firms. They are also employed in the motion picture and television industries, wholesale and retail trade establishments, and public relations firms.

Medical illustrators are employed at hospitals, medical centers and schools, and academic institutions. Laboratories, pharmaceutical companies, publishers of medical and scientific textbooks, and advertising agencies also employ medical illustrators.

Fashion illustrators are employed at magazines, newspapers, and catalog companies. They may also be self employed.

Starting Out

Graduates of illustration programs should develop a portfolio of their work to show to prospective employers or clients. Most schools offer career counseling and job placement assistance to their graduates. Job ads and employment agencies are also potential sources for locating work.

Medical illustrators can also find job placement assistance with the Association of Medical Illustrators (AMI). Joining the AMI is helpful for beginning medical illustrators, and many employers prefer to hire illustrators who have also been certified by the AMI.

Advancement

After an illustrator gains experience, he or she will be given more challenging and unusual work. Those with strong computer skills will have the best chances for advancement. Illustrators can advance by developing skills in a specialized area, or even starting their own business. Illustrators can also go into teaching, in colleges and universities at the undergraduate and graduate levels.

Earnings

The pay for illustrations can be as little as a byline, though in the beginning of your career it may be worth it just to get exposure. Some illustrators can earn several thousand dollars for a single work. Freelance work is often insecure because of the fluctuation in pay rates and steadiness of work. The U.S. Department of Labor reports that median earnings for salaried visual artists, who usually work full-time, were about $31,690 a year in 1998. The middle 50 percent earned between $23,790 and $41,980 a year. The top 10 percent earned more than $64,580 and the bottom 10 percent earned less than $17,910.

Illustrators generally receive good benefits, including health and life insurance, pension plans, vacation, sick, and holiday pay.

Work Environment

Illustrators generally work in clean, well-lit offices. They spend a great deal of time at their desks, whether in front of a computer or at the drafting table. Medical illustrators are sometimes required to visit operating rooms and other health care settings. Fashion illustrators may be required to attend fashion shows and other industry events. Because the fashion world is extremely competitive and fast-paced, fashion illustrators tend to work long hours under the pressure of deadlines and demanding personalities.

Outlook

Employment of visual artists is expected to grow faster than the average for all occupations through the year 2008, according to the *Occupational Outlook Handbook*. The growth of the Internet should provide opportunities for illustrators, although the increased use of computer-aided design systems is a threat because operators do not necessarily need artistic talent or training.

The employment outlook for medical illustrators is very good. Because there are only a few graduate programs in medical illustration, and small graduation classes, medical illustrators will find great demand for their skills. The field of medicine and science in general is always growing, and medical illustrators will be needed to depict new techniques, procedures, and discoveries.

The outlook for careers in fashion illustration is dependent on the businesses of magazine publishing and advertising. Growth of advertising and public relations agencies will provide new jobs. The popularity of American fashion in other parts of the world will also create a demand for fashion illustrators to provide the artwork needed to sell to a global market.

For More Information

The following national institution promotes and stimulates interest in the art of illustration by offering exhibits, lectures, educational programs, and social exchange.
Society of Illustrators
128 East 63rd Street
New York, NY 10021-7303
Tel: 212-838-2560
Email: SI1901@aol.com
Web: http://www.societyillustrators.org

For information on educational and career opportunities for medical illustrators, contact:
Association of Medical Illustrators
2965 Flowers Road South, Suite 105
Atlanta, GA 30341
Tel: 770-454-7933
Email: assnhq@mindspring.com
Web: http://medical-illustrators.org

For information on membership, contact:
Guild of Natural Science Illustrators
> PO Box 652
> Ben Franklin Station
> Washington, DC 20044-0652
> Tel: 301-309-1514
> Web: http://pw1.netcom.com/~roses/gnsi/

This organization is committed to improving conditions for all creators of graphic art and to raising standards for the entire industry.
Graphic Artists Guild
> 90 John Street, Suite 403
> New York, NY 10038-3202
> Tel: 800-500-2672
> Email: execdir@gag.org
> Web: http://www.gag.org

This college offers programs in fashion design and advertising and design.
International Academy of Merchandising and Design
> 1 North State Street, 4th Floor
> Chicago, IL 60602
> Tel: 877-ACADEMY (222-3369)
> Web: http://www.iamd.edu

Management Analysts and Consultants

Overview

Management analysts and consultants *analyze business or operating procedures to devise the most efficient methods of accomplishing work. They gather and organize information about operating problems and procedures and prepare recommendations for implementing new systems or changes. They may update manuals outlining established methods of performing work and train personnel in new applications.*

The Job

Management analysts and consultants are called in to solve any of a vast array of organizational problems. They are often needed when a rapidly growing small company needs a better system of control over inventories and expenses.

The role of the consultant is to come into a situation in which a client is unsure or inexpert and to recommend actions or provide assessments. There are many different types of management analysts and consultants. In general, they all require knowledge of general management, operations, marketing, logistics, materials management and physical distribution, finance and accounting, human resources, electronic data processing and systems, and management science.

Management analysts and consultants may be called in when a major manufacturer must reorganize its corporate structure when acquiring a new division. For example, they assist when a company relocates to another state by coordinating the move, planning the new facility, and training new workers.

The work of management analysts and consultants is quite flexible—it varies from job to job. In general, management analysts and consultants collect, review, and analyze data, make recommendations, and assist in the implementation of their proposals. Some projects require several consultants to work together, each specializing in a different area. Other jobs require the analysts to work independently.

Public and private organizations use management analysts for a variety of reasons. Some don't have adequate resources to handle a project. Others, before they pursue a particular course of action, will consult an analyst to determine what resources will be required or what problems will be encountered. Some organizations are seeking outside advice on how to resolve organizational problems that have already been identified or to avoid troublesome problems that could arise.

Firms providing consulting practitioners range in size from solo practitioners to large international organizations employing hundreds of people. The services are generally provided on a contract basis. A company will choose a consulting firm that specializes in the area that needs assistance, and then the two firms negotiate the conditions of the contract. Contract variables include the proposed cost of the project, staffing requirements, and deadline.

After getting a contract, the analyst's first job is to define the nature and extent of the project. He or she analyzes statistics, such as annual revenues, employment, or expenditures. He or she may also interview employees and observe the operations of the organization on a day-to-day basis.

The next step for the analyst is to use his or her knowledge of management systems to develop solutions. While preparing recommendations, he or she must take into account the general nature of the business, the relationship of the firm to others in its industry, the firm's internal organization, and the information gained through their data collection and analysis.

Once they have decided on a course of action, management analysts and consultants usually write reports of their findings and recommendations and present them to the client. They often make formal oral presentations about their findings as well. Some projects require only reports; others require assistance in implementing the suggestions.

Requirements

Employers generally prefer to hire management analysts and consultants with a master's degree in business or public administration, or at least a bachelor's degree and several years of appropriate work experience. Most government agencies offer entry-level analyst and consultant positions to people with bachelor's degrees and no work experience. Many entrants are also career changers who were formerly mid- and upper-level managers. With half the practicing management consultants self-employed, career changing is a common route into the field.

High School

High school courses that will give you a general preparation for this field include business, mathematics, and computer science. Management analysts and consultants must pass on their findings through written or oral presentations, so be sure to take English and speech classes, too.

Postsecondary Training

Many fields of study provide a suitable formal educational background for this occupation because of the diversity of problem areas addressed by management analysts and consultants. These include many areas in the computer and information sciences, engineering, business and management, education, communications, marketing and distribution, and architecture and environmental design.

When hired directly from school, management analysts and consultants often participate in formal company training programs. These programs may include instruction on policies and procedures, computer systems and software, and management practices and principles. Regardless of background, most management analysts and consultants routinely attend conferences to keep abreast of current developments in the field.

Certification and Licensing

The Institute of Management Consultants offers the Certified Management Consultant (CMC) designation to those who pass an examination and meet minimum educational and experience criteria. Certification is voluntary, but may provide an additional advantage to job seekers.

Other Requirements

Management analysts and consultants are often responsible for recommending layoffs of staff, so it is important that they learn to deal with people diplomatically. Their job requires a great deal of tact, enlisting cooperation while exerting leadership, debating their points, and pointing out errors. Consultants must be quick thinkers, able to refute objections with finality. They also must be able to make excellent presentations.

A management analyst must be unbiased and analytical, with a disposition toward the intellectual side of business and a natural curiosity about the way things work best.

Exploring

The reference departments of most libraries include business areas that will have valuable research tools such as encyclopedias of business consultants and "who's who" of business consultants. These books should list management analysis and consulting firms across the country, describing their annual sales and area of specialization, like industrial, high tech, small business, and retail. Interested students can call or write to these firms and ask for more information.

Employers

About 55 percent of all management analysts and consultants are self-employed. Federal, state, and local governments employ many of the others. The Department of Defense employs the majority of those working for the federal government. The remainder work in the private sector for companies providing consulting services. Although management analysts and consultants are found throughout the country, the majority are concentrated in major metropolitan areas.

Starting Out

Anyone with some degree of business expertise or an expert field can begin to work as a consultant. The number of one- and two-person consulting firms in this country is well over 100,000. Establishing a wide range of appropriate personal contacts is by far the most effective way to get started in this field. Consultants have to sell themselves and their expertise, a task far tougher than selling a tangible product the customer can see and handle. Many consultants get their first clients by advertising in newspapers, magazines, and trade or professional periodicals. After some time in the field, word-of-mouth advertising is often the primary force.

Thousands of business school professors work part-time as management analysts or consultants, entering on the basis of their academic achievement.

Others enter the field through accounting firms known as management consulting services. Others begin as in-house consultants, working for organizations that have their own management consulting operations.

Advancement

A new consultant in a large firm may be referred to as an associate for the first couple of years. The next progression is to *senior associate,* a title that indicates three to five years experience and the ability to supervise others and do more complex and independent work. After about five years, the analyst who is progressing well may become an *engagement manager* with the responsibility to lead a consulting team on a particular client project. The best managers become *senior engagement managers,* leading several study teams or a very large project team. After about seven years, those who excel will be considered for appointment as *junior partners* or *principals.* Partnership involves responsibility for marketing the firm and leading client projects. Some may be promoted to senior partnership or director, but few people successfully run this full course. Management analysts and consultants with entrepreneurial ambition may open their own firms.

Earnings

In 1998, management analysts and consultants earned median earnings of $49,470, according to the *Occupational Outlook Handbook.* The lowest 10 percent earned less than $31,800; the highest 10 percent earned more than $88,470. Salaries and hourly rates for management analysts and consultants vary widely, according to experience, specialization, education, and employer. Analysts and consultants working in the management and public relations industries earned median annual earnings of $57,200 in 1997, while those employed in the computer and data processing services industry earned $47,500.

Management analysts and consultants employed by the federal government earned median annual salaries of $56,400 in 1997; by state government (except education and hospitals), $39,600; and by local government (except education and hospitals), $47,500.

Many consultants can demand between $400 and $1,000 per day. Their fees are often well over $40 per hour. Self-employed management consultants receive no fringe benefits and generally have to maintain their own office, but their pay is usually much higher than salaried consultants. They can make more than $2,000 per day or $250,000 in one year from consulting just two days per week.

Typical benefits for salaried analysts and consultants include health and life insurance, retirement plans, vacation and sick leave, profit sharing, and bonuses for outstanding work. All travel expenses are generally reimbursed by the employer.

Work Environment

Management analysts and consultants generally divide their time between their own offices and the client's office or production facility. They can spend a great deal of time on the road.

Most management analysts and consultants work at least 40 hours per week plus overtime depending on the project. The nature of consulting projects—working on location with a single client toward a specific goal—allows these professionals to totally immerse themselves in their work. They sometimes work 14- to 16-hour days, and 6- or 7-day work-weeks can be fairly common.

While self-employed, consultants may enjoy the luxury of setting their own hours and doing a great deal of their work at home; the trade-off is sacrificing the benefits provided by the large firms. Their livelihood depends on the additional responsibility of maintaining and expanding their clientele on their own.

Although those in this career usually avoid much of the potential tedium of working for one company all day, every day, they face many pressures resulting from deadlines and client expectations. Because the clients are generally paying generous fees, they want to see dramatic results, and the management analyst can feel the weight of this.

Outlook

Through the year 2008, employment of management analysts is expected to grow faster than the average for all occupations, according to the U.S. Department of Labor. Industry and government agencies are expected to rely more and more on the expertise of these professionals to improve and streamline the performance of their organizations. Many job openings will result from the need to replace personnel who transfer to other fields or leave the labor force.

The challenging nature of this job, coupled with high salary potential, attracts many. A graduate degree, experience and expertise in the industry, as well as a knack for public relations, are needed to stay competitive.

For More Information

For information on certification, contact:
Association of Internal Management Consultants
    19 Harrison St.
    Framingham, MA 01702
    Tel: 508-820-3434
    Email: aimc@resource-network.com
    Web: http://aimc.org/

For industry information, contact the following organizations:
American Management Association
　　1601 Broadway
　　New York, NY 10019-7420
　　Web: http://www.amanet.org/

American Institute of Certified Public Accountants
　　Management Consulting Services Division
　　1211 Avenue of the Americas
　　New York, NY 10036-8775
　　Web: http://www.aicpa.org/

Association of Management Consulting Firms
　　380 Lexington Avenue, Suite 1700
　　New York, NY 10168
　　Tel: 212-551-7887
　　Email: info@amcf.org
　　Web: http://www.amcf.org/

For information on certification, contact:
Institute of Management Consultants
　　1200 19th Street, NW, Suite 300
　　Washington, DC 20036-2422
　　Tel: 202-857-5334
　　Web: http://www.imcusa.org

Paralegals

Overview

Paralegals, *also known as* legal assistants, *assist in trial preparations, investigate facts, prepare documents such as affidavits and pleadings, and, in general, do work customarily performed by lawyers. Paralegals work in law firms, businesses, and government agencies all over the United States; the majority work with lawyers and legislators.*

The Job

A paralegal's main duty is to do everything a lawyer needs to do but doesn't have time to do. Paralegals assist lawyers in a variety of ways to accomplish this goal. Although the lawyer assumes responsibility for the paralegal's work, the paralegal may take on all the duties of the lawyer except for setting fees, appearing in court, accepting cases, and giving legal advice.

Paralegals spend much of their time in law libraries, researching laws and previous cases and compiling facts to help lawyers prepare for trial. Paralegals often interview witnesses as part of their research as well. After analyzing the laws and facts that have been compiled for a particular client, the paralegal often writes a report that the lawyer may use to determine how to proceed with the case. If a case is brought to trial, the paralegal helps prepare legal arguments and draft pleadings to be filed in court. They also organize and store files and correspondence related to cases.

Not all paralegal work centers on trials. Many paralegals work for corporations, agencies, schools, and financial institutions. Paralegals working in business create and maintain contracts, mortgages, affidavits, and other documents. They assist with corporate matters, such as shareholder agreements, contracts, and employee benefit plans. Another important part of a *corporate paralegal's* job is to stay on top of new laws and regulations to make sure the company is operating within those parameters.

Some paralegals work for the government. They may prepare complaints or talk to employers to find out why health or safety standards are not being met. They often analyze legal documents, collect evidence for hearings, and prepare explanatory material on various laws for use by the public. For example, a *court administrator paralegal* is in charge of keeping the courthouse functioning—tasks include monitoring personnel, handling the case load for the court, and general administration.

Other paralegals are involved in community or public-service work. They may help specific groups, such as poor or elderly members of the community. They may file forms, research laws, and prepare documents. They may represent clients at hearings, although they may not appear in court on behalf of a client.

Many paralegals work for large law firms, agencies, and corporations and specialize in a particular area of law. Some work for smaller firms and have a general knowledge of many areas of law. Paralegals have varied duties, and an increasing number use computers in their work.

Requirements

Requirements for paralegals vary by employer. Some paralegals start out as legal secretaries or clerical workers and gradually are given more training and responsibility. The majority, however, choose formal training and education programs.

High School

High school students should take a broad range of subjects, including English, social studies, computer science, and languages, especially Spanish and Latin. Because legal terminology is used constantly, word origins and vocabulary should be a focus.

Postsecondary Training

Formal training programs usually range from 1 to 3 years and are offered in a variety of educational settings: 4-year colleges and universities, law schools, community and junior colleges, business schools, proprietary schools, and paralegal associations. Admission requirements vary, but good grades in high school and college are always an asset. There are over 800 paralegal programs, about 232 of which have been approved by the American Bar Association.

Some paralegal programs require a bachelor's degree for admission; others do not require any college. In either case, those who have a college degree usually have an edge over those who do not.

Certification or Licensing

Paralegals are not required to be licensed or certified. Instead, when lawyers employ paralegals, they often follow guidelines designed to protect the public from the practice of law by unqualified persons.

Paralegals may, however, opt to be certified. To do so, they may take and pass an extensive two-day test conducted by the National Association of Legal Assistants Certifying Board. Paralegals who pass the test may use the title Certified Legal Assistant (CLA) after their names. In 1996, the National Federation of Paralegal Associations established the Paralegal Advanced Competency Exam, a means for paralegals with bachelor's degrees and at least two years' experience to acquire professional recognition. Paralegals who pass this exam may use the designation Registered Paralegal (RP).

Other Requirements

Communication skills, both verbal and written, are vital to working as a paralegal. The paralegal must be able to turn research into reports that a lawyer or corporate executive can use. A paralegal must be able to think logically and learn new laws and regulations quickly. Research skills, computer skills, and people skills are necessary for success as a paralegal.

Exploring

If you're interested in a career as a paralegal, but you aren't positive yet, don't worry. There are several ways you can explore the career of a paralegal. Colleges, universities, and technical schools have a wealth of information available for the asking. Elizabeth Houser, a practicing paralegal, says "Contact schools that have paralegal programs and ask questions; they are helpful and will give you a lot of information about being a paralegal."

Look for summer or part-time employment as a secretary or in the mailroom of a law firm to get an idea of the nature of the work. If paid positions aren't available, offer yourself as a volunteer to the law offices in town. Ask your guidance counselor to help you set up a volunteer/internship agreement with a lawyer.

Talk to your history or government teacher about organizing a trip to a lawyer's office and a courthouse. Ask your teacher to set aside time for you to talk to paralegals working there and to their supervising attorneys.

If you have access to a computer, search the World Wide Web for information on student organizations that are affiliated with the legal profession. You can also write to the organizations listed at the end of this article for general information.

Employers

A majority of paralegals work for lawyers in law offices or in law firms. Other paralegals work for the government, namely for the Federal Trade Commission, Justice Department, Treasury, Internal Revenue Service, Department of the Interior, and many other agencies and offices.

Paralegals are also found in the business community. Anywhere legal matters are part of the day-to-day work, paralegals are usually handling them. Paralegals fit in well in business because many smaller corporations must deal with legal regulations but don't necessarily need an attorney or a team of lawyers.

Paralegals in business can be found all over the country. Larger cities employ more paralegals who focus on the legal side of the profession, and government paralegals will find the most opportunities in state capitals and Washington, DC.

Starting Out

Although some law firms promote legal secretaries to paralegal status, most employers prefer to hire individuals who have completed paralegal programs. To have the best opportunity at getting a quality job in the paralegal field, you should attend a paralegal school. In addition to providing a solid background in paralegal studies, most schools help graduates find jobs. Even though the job market for paralegals is expected to grow rapidly over the next 10 years, those with the best credentials will get the best jobs.

For Elizabeth, the internship program was the springboard to her first paralegal position. "The paralegal program of study I took required an internship. I was hired directly from that internship experience."

The National Federation of Paralegal Associations recommends using job banks that are sponsored by paralegal associations across the country. For paralegal associations that may be able to help, see the addresses listed at the end of this article.

Many jobs for paralegals are posted on the Internet as well. Search on the phrase "paralegals and jobs" to see what positions are available.

Advancement

There are no formal advancement paths for paralegals; paralegals usually do not become lawyers or judges. There are, however, some possibilities for advancement, as large firms are beginning to establish career programs for paralegals.

For example, a person may be promoted from a paralegal to a head legal assistant who supervises others. In addition, a paralegal may specialize in one area of law, such as environmental, real estate, or medical malpractice. Many paralegals also advance by moving from small to large firms.

Expert paralegals who specialize in one area of law may go into business for themselves. Rather than work for one firm, these freelance paralegals often contract their services to many lawyers. Some paralegals with bachelor's degrees enroll in law school to train to become lawyers.

Paralegals can also move horizontally by taking their specialized knowledge of the law into another field, such as insurance, occupational health, or law enforcement.

Earnings

Salaries vary greatly for paralegals. The size and location of the firm and the education and experience of the employee are some factors that determine the annual earnings of paralegals.

According to 1997 statistics from the National Federation of Paralegal Associations, beginning paralegals average about $30,700 a year. Paralegals with 7 to 10 years' experience earn about $34,000. Top paralegals in large offices can earn as much as $40,000 a year, and paralegal supervisors, $40,000 to $50,000. Many paralegals receive year-end bonuses, some averaging $2,100 or more.

Paralegals employed by the federal government averaged $43,900 annually in 1997, as reported by the U.S. Department of Labor.

Work Environment

Paralegals often work in pleasant and comfortable offices. Much of their work is performed in a law library. Some paralegals work out of their homes in special situations. When investigation is called for, paralegals may travel to gather information. Most paralegals work a 40-hour week, although long hours are sometimes required to meet court-imposed deadlines. Longer hours—sometimes as much as 90 hours per week—are usually the normal routine for paralegals starting out in law offices and firms.

Many of the paralegal's duties involve routine tasks, so they must have a great deal of patience. However, paralegals may be given increasingly difficult assignments over time. Paralegals are often unsupervised, especially as they gain experience and a reputation for quality work. Elizabeth does much of her work unsupervised. "You get to put a lot of yourself into what you do and that provides a high level of job satisfaction," she says.

Outlook

In 1998, there were about 136,000 paralegals employed in the United States; most were employed by private law firms. The employment outlook for paralegals through 2008 is excellent; the career of paralegal is one of the fastest-growing professions in the country. One reason for the expected growth in the profession is the financial benefits of employing paralegals. The paralegal, whose duties fall between those of the legal secretary and those of the attorney, helps make the delivery of legal services more cost effective to clients. The growing need for legal services among the general population and the increased popularity of prepaid legal plans is creating a tremendous demand for paralegals in private law firms. In the private sector, paralegals can work in banks, insurance companies, real estate firms, and corporate legal departments. In the public sector, there is a growing need for paralegals in the courts and community legal service programs, government agencies, and consumer organizations.

The growth of this occupation, to some extent, is dependent on the economy. Businesses are less likely to pursue litigation cases when profit margins are down, thus curbing the need for new hires.

For More Information

For information regarding accredited educational facilities, contact:
American Association for Paralegal Education
2965 Flowers Road South, Suite 105
Atlanta, GA 30341
Tel: 770-452-9877
Email: info@aafpe.org
Web: http://www.aafpe.org

For general information about careers in the law field, contact:
American Bar Association
750 North Lake Shore Drive
Chicago, IL 60611
Tel: 312-988-5000
Email: info@abanet.org
Web: http://www.abanet.org

For information about educational and licensing programs, certification, and paralegal careers, contact:
National Association of Legal Assistants
1516 South Boston Avenue, Suite 200
Tulsa, OK 74119
Tel: 918-587-6828
Email: nala@nala.org
Web: http://www.nala.org

For brochures about almost every aspect of becoming a paralegal, contact:
National Federation of Paralegal Associations
PO Box 33108
Kansas City, MO 64114-0108
Tel: 816-941-4000
Email: info@paralegals.org
Web: http://www.paralegals.org

For information about employment networks and school listings, contact:
National Paralegal Association
PO Box 406
Solebury, PA 18963
Tel: 215-297-8333
Email: admin@nationalparalegal.org
Web: http://www.nationalparalegal.org

For various career information, contact:
Association of Legal Administrators
175 East Hawthorn Parkway, Suite 325
Vernon Hills, IL 60061-1428
Tel: 847-816-1212
Web: http://www.alanet.org

Physicians

Physicians *diagnose, prescribe medicines for, and otherwise treat diseases and disorders of the human body. A physician may also perform surgery and often specializes in one aspect of medical care and treatment. Physicians hold either a doctor of medicine (M.D.) or osteopathic medicine (D.O.) degree.*

The Job

The greatest number of physicians are in private practice. They see patients by appointment in their offices and examining rooms, and visit patients who are confined to the hospital. In the hospital, they may perform operations or give other kinds of medical treatment. Some physicians also make calls on patients at home if the patient is not able to get to the physician's office or if the illness is an emergency.

Approximately 15 percent of physicians in private practice are *general practitioners* or *family practitioners.* They see patients of all ages and both sexes and will diagnose and treat those ailments that are not severe enough or unusual enough to require the services of a specialist. When special problems arise, however, the general practitioner will refer the patient to a specialist.

Not all physicians are engaged in private practice. Some are in academic medicine and teach in medical schools or teaching hospitals. Some are engaged only in research. Some are salaried employees of health maintenance organizations or other prepaid health care plans. Some are salaried hospital employees.

Some physicians, often called *medical officers,* are employed by the federal government, in such positions as public health, or in the service of the Department of Veterans Affairs. State and local governments also employ physicians for public health agency work. A large number of physicians serve with the armed forces, both in this country and overseas.

Industrial physicians or *occupational physicians* are employed by large industrial firms for two main reasons: to prevent illnesses that may be caused by certain kinds of work and to treat accidents or illnesses of employees. Although most industrial physicians may roughly be classified as general practitioners because of the wide variety of illnesses that they must recognize and treat, their knowledge must also extend to public health techniques and to understanding such relatively new hazards as radiation and the toxic effects of various chemicals, including insecticides.

A specialized type of industrial or occupational physician is the flight surgeon. *Flight surgeons* study the effects of high-altitude flying on the physical condition of flight personnel. They place members of the flight staff in special low-pressure and refrigeration chambers that simulate high-altitude conditions and study the reactions on their blood pressure, pulse and respiration rate, and body temperature.

Another growing specialty is the field of nuclear medicine. Some large hospitals have a nuclear research laboratory, which functions under the direction of a *chief of nuclear medicine,* who coordinates the activities of the lab with other hospital departments and medical personnel. These physicians perform tests using nuclear isotopes and use techniques that let physicians see and understand organs deep within the body.

M.D.s may become specialists in any of the 40 different medical care specialties.

Requirements

High School

The physician is required to devote many years to study before being admitted to practice. Interested high school students should enroll in a college preparatory course, and take courses in English, languages (especially Latin), the humanities, social studies, and mathematics, in addition to courses in biology, chemistry, and physics.

Postsecondary Training

The student who hopes to enter medicine should be admitted first to a liberal arts program in an accredited undergraduate institution. Some colleges offer a "premedical" course, and it is advisable for the student to take such a course where it is offered. A good general education, however, with as many courses as possible in science and perhaps a major in biology, is considered adequate preparation for the study of medicine. Courses should include physics, biology, inorganic and organic chemistry, English, mathematics, and the social sciences.

College freshmen who hope to apply to a medical school early in their senior year should have adequate knowledge of the requirements for admission to one of the 125 accredited schools of medicine or 19 accredited schools of osteopathic medicine in the country. They should consult a copy of *Medical School Admission Requirements, U.S. and Canada,* available from the Association of American Medical Colleges. It is also available in college libraries. If students read carefully the admissions requirements of the several medical schools to which they hope to apply, they will avoid making mistakes in choosing a graduate program.

Students who do not enter a premedical program may find it possible to change to a major in biology or chemistry after they have enrolled. Such majors may make them eligible for consideration to be admitted to many medical schools.

Some students may be admitted to medical school after only three years of study in an undergraduate program. There are a few medical schools that will award the bachelor's degree at the end of the first year of medical school study. This practice is becoming less common as more students seek admission to medical schools. Most premedical students plan to spend four years in an undergraduate program and to receive the bachelor's degree before entering the four-year medical school program.

During the second or third year in college, undergraduates should arrange with an advisor to take the Medical College Admission Test (MCAT). This test is given each spring and each fall at certain selected sites. The student's advisor should know the date, place, and time; or the student may write for this information to the Association of American Medical Colleges. All medical colleges in this country require this test for admission, and a student's MCAT score is one of the factors that is weighed in the decision to accept or reject any applicant. Because the test does not evaluate medical knowledge, most college students who are enrolled in liberal arts programs should not find it to be unduly difficult. The examination covers four areas: verbal facility, quantitative ability, knowledge of the humanities and social sciences, and knowledge of biology, chemistry, and physics.

Students who hope to be admitted to medical school are encouraged to apply to at least three institutions to increase their chances of being accepted by one of them. Approximately one out of every two qualified applicants to medical schools will be admitted each year. To facilitate this process, the American Medical College Application Service (AMCAS) will check, copy, and submit applications to medical schools specified by the individual student. More information about this service may be obtained from AMCAS, premedical advisers, and medical schools.

In addition to the traditional medical schools, there are several schools of basic medical sciences that enroll medical students for the first two years (preclinical experience) of medical school. They offer a preclinical curriculum to students similar to that which is offered by a regular medical school. At the end of the two-year program, the student will then apply to a four-year medical school for the final two years of instruction.

Although high scholarship is a determining factor in admitting a student to a medical school, it is actually only one of the criteria considered. By far the greatest number of successful applicants to medical schools are "B" students. Because admission is also determined by a number of other factors, including a personal interview, other qualities in addition to a high scholastic average are considered desirable for a prospective physician. High on the list of desirable qualities are emotional stability, integrity, reliability, resourcefulness, and a sense of service.

The average student enters medical school at age 21 or 22. The student then begins another four years of formal schooling. During the first two years of medical school, the student learns human anatomy, biochemistry, physiology, pharmacology, psychology, microbiology, pathology, medical ethics, and laws governing medicine. Most instruction in the first two years is given through classroom lectures, laboratories, seminars, independent research, and the reading of textbook material and other types of literature. Students also learn to take medical histories, examine patients, and recognize symptoms.

During the last two years in medical school, the student becomes actively involved in the treatment process. Students spend a large proportion of the time in the hospital as part of a medical team headed by a teaching physician who specializes in a particular area. Others on the team may be interns or residents. Students are closely supervised as they learn techniques such as how to take a patient's medical history, how to make a physical examination, how to work in the laboratory, how to make a diagnosis, and how to keep all the necessary records.

Students rotate from one medical specialty to another, to obtain a broad understanding of each field. They are assigned to duty in internal medicine, pediatrics, psychiatry, obstetrics and gynecology, and surgery. Students may be assigned to other specialties, too.

In addition to this hospital work, students continue to take coursework. They are expected to be responsible for assigned studies and also for some independent study.

Most states require all new M.D.s to complete at least one year of postgraduate training, and a few require an internship plus a one-year residency. Physicians wishing to specialize spend from three to seven years in advanced residency training plus another two or more years of practice in the specialty. Then they must pass a specialty board examination to become a board-certified M.D. The residency years are stressful: residents often work 24-hour shifts and put in 80 hours or more per week.

For a teaching or research career, physicians may also earn a master's degree or a Ph.D. in biochemistry or microbiology.

Certification or Licensing

After receiving the M.D. degree, the new physician is required to take an examination to be licensed to practice. Every state requires such an examination. It is conducted through the board of medical examiners in each state. Some states have reciprocity agreements with other states so that a physician licensed in one state may be automatically licensed in another without being required to pass another examination. Because this is not true throughout the United States, however, the wise physician will find out about licensing procedures before planning to move.

Other Requirements

Prospective physicians must have some plan for financing their long and costly education. They face a period of at least eight years after college when they will not be self-supporting. While still in school, students may be able to work only during summer vacations, because the necessary laboratory courses of the regular school year are so time consuming that little time is left for activities other than the preparation of daily lessons. Some scholarships and loans are available to qualified students.

Physicians who work directly with patients need to have great sensitivity to their needs. Interpersonal skills are required by all physicians, even in isolated research laboratories, since they must work and communicate with other scientists. Since new technology and discoveries happen at such a rapid rate, physicians must continually pursue further education to keep up with new treatments, tools, and medicines.

Exploring

One of the best introductions to a career in health care is to volunteer at a local hospital, clinic, or nursing home. In this way it is possible to get a feel for what it's like to work around other health care professionals and patients and possibly determine exactly where your interests lie. As in any career, reading as much as possible about the profession, talking with a high school counselor, and interviewing those working in the field are other important ways to explore your interest.

Employers

Physicians can find employment in a wide variety of settings, including hospitals, nursing homes, managed-care offices, prisons, schools and universities, research laboratories, trauma centers, clinics, and public health centers. Some are self-employed in their own or group practices. In the past, many physicians went into business for themselves, either by starting their own practice or by becoming a partner in an existing one. Very few physicians—about 6 percent—are choosing to follow this path today. There are a number of reasons for this shift. Often, the costs of starting a practice or buying into an existing practice are too high. Most are choosing to take salaried positions with hospitals or groups of physicians.

Jobs for physicians are available all over the world, although licensing requirements may vary. In Third World countries, there is great demand for medical professionals of all types. Conditions, supplies, and equipment may be poor and pay is minimal, but there are great rewards in terms of experience. Many doctors fulfill part or all of their residency requirements by practicing in other countries.

Physicians interested in teaching may find employment at medical schools or university hospitals. There are also positions available in government agencies such as the Centers for Disease Control, the National Institutes of Health, and the Food and Drug Administration.

Pharmaceutical companies and chemical companies hire physicians to research and develop new drugs, instruments, and procedures.

Starting Out

There are no shortcuts to entering the medical profession. Requirements are an M.D. degree, a licensing examination, a one- or two-year internship, and a period of residency that may extend as long as five years.

Upon completing this program, which may take up to 15 years, physicians are then ready to enter practice. They may choose to open a solo private practice, enter a partnership practice, enter a group practice, or take a salaried job with a managed-care facility or hospital. Salaried positions are also available with federal and state agencies, the military, including the Department of Veterans Affairs, and private companies. Teaching and research jobs are usually obtained after other experience is acquired.

The highest ratio of physicians to patients is in the Northeast and West. The lowest ratio is in the South. Most M.D.s practice in urban areas near hospitals and universities.

Advancement

Physicians who work in a managed-care setting or for a large group or corporation can advance by opening a private practice. The average physician in private practice does not advance in the accustomed sense of the word. Their progress consists of advancing in skill and understanding, in numbers of patients, and in income. They may be made a fellow in a professional specialty or elected to an important office in the American Medical Association or American Osteopathic Association. Teaching and research positions may also increase a physician's status.

Some physicians may become directors of a laboratory, managed-care facility, hospital department, or medical school program. Some may move into hospital administration positions.

A physician can achieve recognition by conducting research in new medicines, treatments, and cures, and publishing their findings in medical journals. Participation in professional organizations can also bring prestige.

A physician can advance by pursuing further education in a subspecialty or a second field such as biochemistry or microbiology.

Earnings

Physicians have among the highest average earnings of any occupational group. The level of income for any individual physician depends on a number of factors, such as region of the country, economic status of the patients, and the physician's specialty, skill, experience, professional reputation, and personality. Income tends to vary less across geographic regions, however, than across specialties. The median income after expenses for all physicians in 1997, according to the American Medical Association, was $164,000 per year. The median income of radiologists was $260,000; general surgeons, $217,000; family practitioners, $132,000; anesthesiologists, $220,000, and emergency medicine physicians, $195,000.

In 1998-99, the average first year resident received a stipend of about $34,100 a year, depending on the type of residency, the size of the hospital, and the geographic area. Sixth year residents earned about $42,100 a year. If the physician enters private practice, earnings during the first year may not be impressive. As the patients increase in number, however, earnings will also increase.

Physicians who complete their residencies but have no other experience begin work with the Department of Veterans Affairs at salaries of about $44,400 in addition to other cash benefits of up to $13,000.

Salaried doctors usually earn fringe benefits such as health and dental insurance, paid vacations, and the opportunity to participate in retirement plans.

Work Environment

The offices and examining rooms of most physicians are well equipped, attractive, well lighted, and well ventilated. There is usually at least one nurse-receptionist on the physician's staff, and there may be several nurses, a laboratory technician, one or more secretaries, a bookkeeper, or receptionist.

Physicians usually see patients by appointments that are scheduled according to individual requirements. They may reserve all mornings for hospital visits and surgery. They may see patients in the office only on certain days of the week.

Physicians spend much of their time at the hospital performing surgery, setting fractures, working in the emergency room, or visiting patients.

Physicians in private practice have the advantages of working independently, but most put in long hours—an average of 60 per week in 1998. Also, they may be called from their homes or offices in times of emergency. Telephone calls may come at any hour of the day or night. It is difficult for physicians to plan leisure-time activities, because their plans may change without notice. One of the advantages of group practice is that members of the group rotate emergency duty.

The areas in most need of physicians are rural hospitals and medical centers. Because the physician is normally working alone, and covering a broad territory, the workday can be quite long with little opportunity for vacation. Because placement in rural communities has become so difficult, some towns are providing scholarship money to students who pledge to work in the community for a number of years.

Physicians in academic medicine or in research have regular hours, work under good physical conditions, and often determine their own workload. Teaching and research physicians alike are usually provided with the best and most modern equipment.

Outlook

In 1998, there were about 577,000 M.D.s and D.O.s working in the United States. Others are involved in research, teaching, administration, and consulting for insurance or pharmaceutical companies. About 70 percent of all physicians practice in offices. Others are on the staff of hospitals, or work in a variety of other health care facilities and in schools, prisons, and business firms.

The U.S. Department of Labor reports that this field is expected to grow faster than the average for all other occupations through the year 2008. Population growth, particularly among the elderly, is a factor in the demand for physicians. Another factor contributing to the predicted increase is the widespread availability of medical insurance, through both private plans and public programs. More physicians will also be needed for medical research, public health, rehabilitation, and industrial medicine. New technology will allow physicians to perform more procedures to treat ailments once thought incurable.

Employment opportunities will be good for family practitioners and internists, geriatric and preventive care specialists, as well as general pediatricians. Rural and low-income areas are in need of more physicians, and there is a short supply of general surgeons and psychiatrists.

The shift in health care delivery from hospitals to outpatient centers and other nontraditional settings to contain rising costs may mean that more and more physicians will become salaried employees. In 1994, for example, 39 percent of employed physicians were considered employees, rather than self-employed, up from 36 percent the previous year.

There will be considerable competition among newly trained physicians entering practice, particularly in large cities. Physicians willing to locate to inner cities and rural areas—where physicians are scarce—should encounter little difficulty.

The issue of physician oversupply has been addressed by groups such as the National Academy of Sciences Institute of Medicine and the Pew Health Professions Commission. They suggest limiting the number of future residency positions available to reduce the number of doctors vying for positions in the medical field.

For More Information

Visit the AAFP Web site to access career information, including the online pamphlet, Consider a Career in Family Practice.

American Academy of Family Physicians (AAFP)
      11400 Tomahawk Creek Parkway
      Leawood, KS 66211-2672
      Tel: 913-906-6000
      Email: fp@aafp.org
      Web: http://www.aafp.org

For general information on medical careers, contact:
American Medical Association
      515 North State Street
      Chicago, IL 60610
      Tel: 312-464-5000
      Web: http://www.ama-assn.org

For a list of accredited U.S. and Canadian medical schools and other education information, contact:
Association of American Medical Colleges
      2450 N Street, NW
      Washington, DC 20037-1126
      Tel: 202-828-0400
      Web: http://www.aamc.org

Police Officers

Police officers *perform many duties relating to public safety. Their responsibilities include not only preserving the peace, preventing criminal acts, enforcing the law, investigating crimes, and arresting those who violate the law but also directing traffic, community relations work, and controlling crowds at public events. Police officers are employed at the federal, state, county, and city level.*

State police officers *patrol highways and enforce the laws and regulations that govern the use of those highways, in addition to performing general police work. Police officers are under oath to uphold the law 24 hours a day.*

The Job

If police officers patrol a beat or work in small communities, their duties may be many and varied. In large city departments, their work may be highly specialized.

Depending on the orders they receive from their commanding officers, police may direct traffic during the rush-hour periods and at special events when traffic is unusually heavy. They may patrol public places such as parks, streets, and public gatherings to maintain law and order. Police are sometimes called upon to prevent or break up riots and to act as escorts at funerals, parades, and other public events. They may administer first aid in emergency situations, assist in rescue operations of various kinds, investigate crimes, issue tickets to violators of traffic or parking laws or other regulations, or arrest drunk drivers. Officers in small towns may have to perform all these duties and administrative work as well.

As officers patrol their assigned beats, either on foot, bicycle, horseback, or in cars, they must be alert for any situations that arise and be ready to take appropriate action. Many times they must be alert to identify stolen cars, identify and locate lost children, and identify and apprehend escaped criminals and others wanted by various law enforcement agencies. While on patrol, they keep in constant contact with headquarters and their fellow officers by calling in regularly on two-way radios. Although their profession may at times be dangerous, police officers are trained not to endanger their own lives or the lives of ordinary citizens. If they need assistance, they radio for additional officers.

In large city police departments, officers usually have more specific duties and specialized assignments. The police departments generally are comprised of special work divisions such as communications, criminal investigation, firearms identification, fingerprint identification and forensic science, accident prevention, and administrative services. In very large cities, police departments may have special work units such as the harbor patrol, canine corps, mounted police, vice squad, fraud or bunco squad, traffic control, records control, and rescue units. A few of the job titles for these specialties are identification and records commanders and officers, narcotics and vice detectives or investigators, homicide squad commanding officers, detective chiefs, traffic lieutenants, sergeants, parking enforcement officers, public safety officers, accident-prevention squad officers, safety instruction police officers, and community relations lieutenants.

In very large city police departments, officers may fill positions as police chiefs, precinct sergeants and captains, desk officers, booking officers, police inspectors, identification officers, complaint evaluation supervisors and officers, and crime prevention police officers. Some officers work as plainclothes detectives in criminal investigation divisions. *Internal affairs investigators* are employed to police the police. Other specialized police officers include police reserves commanders; *police officer commanding officers III,* who act as supervisors in missing persons and fugitive investigations; and *police officers III,* who investigate and pursue nonpayment and fraud fugitives. Many police departments employ *police clerks,* who perform administrative and community-oriented tasks.

A major responsibility for *state police officers* (sometimes known as *state troopers* or *highway patrol officers*) is to patrol the highways and enforce the laws and regulations of those traveling on them. Riding in patrol cars equipped with two-way radios, they monitor traffic for troublesome or dangerous situations. They write traffic tickets and issue warnings to drivers who are violating traffic laws or otherwise not observing safe driving practices. They radio for assistance for drivers who are stopped because of breakdowns, flat tires, illnesses, or other reasons. They direct traffic around congested areas caused by fires, road repairs, accidents, and other emergencies. They may check the weight of commercial vehicles to verify that they are within allowable limits, conduct driver examinations, or give safety information to the public.

In case of a highway accident, officers take charge of the activities at the site by directing traffic, giving first aid to any injured parties, and calling for emergency equipment such as ambulances, fire trucks, or tow trucks. They write up a report to be used by investigating officers who attempt to determine the cause of the accident.

In addition to these responsibilities, state police officers in most states do some general police work. They are often the primary law-enforcement agency in communities or counties that have no police force or a large sheriff's department. In those areas, they may investigate such crimes as burglary and assault. They also may assist municipal or county police in capturing lawbreakers or control civil disturbances.

Most police officers are trained in the use of firearms and carry guns. Police in special divisions, such as chemical analysis and handwriting and fingerprint identification, have special training to perform their work. Police officers often testify in court regarding cases with which they have been involved. Police personnel are required to complete accurate and thorough records of their cases.

Requirements

High School

The majority of police departments today require that applicants have a high school education. Although a high school diploma is not always required, related work experience is generally required.

High school students who are interested in pursuing this career will find the subjects of psychology, sociology, English, law, mathematics, U.S. government and history, chemistry, and physics most helpful. Because physical stamina is very important in this work, sports and physical education are also valuable. Knowledge of a foreign language is especially helpful, and bilingual officers are often in great demand. High school students interested in specialized and advanced positions in law enforcement should pursue studies leading to college programs in criminology, criminal law, criminal psychology, or related areas.

Postsecondary Training

The best chance for advancement, however, is for officers with some postsecondary education, and many police departments now require a 2-year or 4-year degree, especially for more specialized areas of police work. There are more than 800 junior colleges and universities offering 2-year and 4-year degree programs in law enforcement. The armed forces also offer training and opportunities in law enforcement that can be applied to civilian police work.

Newly recruited police officers must pass a special training program. After training, they are usually placed on a probationary period lasting from three to six months. In small towns and communities, training may be given on the job by working with an experienced officer. Inexperienced officers are never sent out on patrol alone but are always accompanied by veteran officers.

Large city police departments give classroom instruction in laws, accident investigation, city ordinances, and traffic control. These departments also give instruction in the handling of firearms, methods of apprehension and arrest, self-defense tactics, and first-aid techniques. Both state and municipal police officers are trained in safe driving procedures and maneuvering an automobile at high speeds.

Other Requirements

Police job appointments in most large cities and in many smaller cities and towns are governed by local civil service regulations. Applicants are required to pass written tests designed to measure the candidates' intelligence and general aptitude for police work. Physical examinations are required and usually include tests of physical agility, dexterity, and strength. Candidates' personal histories, backgrounds, and character undergo careful scrutiny because honesty and law-abiding characteristics are essential traits for law-enforcement officers. An important requirement is that the prospective police officer has no arrest record.

Applicants must be at least 21 years of age (or older for some departments), and some municipalities stipulate an age limit of not more than 35 years. Candidates must have, in most cases, 20/20 uncorrected vision, good hearing, and weight proportionate to their height. Applicants must meet locally prescribed weight and height rules for their gender. Most regulations require that applicants be U.S. citizens, and many police departments have residency requirements.

Prospective police officers should enjoy working with people and be able to cooperate with others. Because of the stressful nature of much police work, police officers must be able to think clearly and logically during emergency situations, have a strong degree of emotional control, and be capable of detaching themselves from incidents.

Physical fitness training is a mandatory, continuing activity in most police departments, as are routine physical examinations. Police officers can have no physical disabilities that would prevent them from carrying out their duties.

Exploring

A good way to explore police work is to talk with various law enforcement officers. Most departments have community outreach programs and many have recruiting programs as well. Students may also wish to visit colleges offering programs in police work or write for information on their training programs.

In some cases, high school graduates can explore this occupation by seeking employment as police cadets in large city police departments. These cadets are paid employees who work part time in clerical and other duties. They attend training courses in police science on a part-time basis. When they reach the age of 21, they are eligible to apply for regular police work. Some police departments also hire college students as interns.

Employers

Most police officers work for local governments, with some finding employment with a state department, and a small percentage working for a federal agency. The United States has more than 18,000 municipal police agencies, 3,000 county sheriff departments, and 1,200 state and federal police agencies. In the 1990s, local police departments employed about 604,000 full-time sworn police officers with general arrest powers. Large cities each employ thousands of police officers. In 1997, New York had 31,000 police officers, and Chicago employed nearly 13,000 police officers.

Starting Out

Applicants interested in police work should apply directly to local civil service offices or examining boards to qualify as a candidate for police officer. In some locations, written examinations may be given to groups at specified times. In smaller communities that do not follow civil service methods, applicants should apply directly to the police department or city government offices in the communities where they reside. Those interested in becoming state police officers may apply directly to their state civil service commissions or state police headquarters, which are usually located in the state capital.

Advancement

Advancement in these occupations is determined by several factors. An officer's eligibility for promotion may depend on a specified length of service, job performance, formal education and training courses, and results of written examinations. Those who become eligible for promotion are listed on the promotional list along with other qualified candidates. Promotions generally become available from six months to three years after starting, depending on the department. As positions of different or higher rank become open, candidates are promoted to fill them according to their position on the list. Lines of promotion usually begin with officer third grade and progress to grade two and grade one. Other possible promotional opportunities include the ranks of detective, sergeant, lieutenant, or captain. Many promotions require additional training and testing. Advancement to the very top-ranking positions, such as division, bureau, or department director or chief, may be made by direct political appointment. Most of these top positions are held by officers who have come up through the ranks.

Large city police departments offer the greatest number of advancement opportunities. Most of the larger departments maintain separate divisions, which require administration workers, line officers, and more employees in general at each rank level. Officers may move into areas that they find challenging, such as criminal investigation or forensics.

Most city police departments offer various types of in-service study and training programs. These programs allow police departments to keep up-to-date on the latest police science techniques and are often required for those who want to be considered for promotion. Training courses are provided by police academies, colleges, and other educational institutions. Some of the subjects offered are civil defense, foreign languages, and forgery detection. Some municipal police departments share the cost with their officers or pay all educational expenses if the officers are willing to work toward a college degree in either police work or police administration. Independent study is also often required.

Intensive 12-week administrative training courses are offered by the National Academy of the Federal Bureau of Investigation in Washington, DC. A limited number of officers are selected to participate in this training program.

Advancement opportunities on police forces in small communities are considerably more limited by the rank and number of police personnel needed. Other opportunities for advancement may be found in related police, protective, and security service work with private companies, state and county agencies, and other institutions.

Earnings

According to the U.S. Department of Labor, police officers earned an annual average salary of $37,710 in 1998; the lowest 10 percent earned less than

$22,270 a year, while the highest 10 percent earned over $63,530 annually. Police officers in supervisory positions earned median salaries of $48,700 a year in 1998, with a low of $28,780 and a high of over $84,710. Sheriffs and other law enforcement officers earned median annual salaries of $28,270 in 1998. Salaries for police officers range widely based on geographic location. Police departments in the West and North generally pay more than those in the South.

Most police officers receive periodic and annual salary increases up to a limit set for their rank and length of service. Police departments generally pay special compensation to cover the cost of uniforms. They usually provide any equipment required such as firearms and handcuffs. Overtime pay may be given for certain work shifts or emergency duty. In these instances, officers are usually paid straight or time-and-a-half pay, while extra time off is sometimes given as compensation.

Because most police officers are civil service employees, they receive generous benefits, including health insurance and paid vacation and sick leave, and enjoy increased job security. In addition, most police departments offer retirement plans and retirement after 20 or 25 years of service, usually at half pay.

Work Environment

Police officers work under many different types of circumstances. Much of their work may be performed outdoors, as they ride in patrol cars or walk the beats assigned to them. In emergency situations, no consideration can be made for weather conditions, time of day or night, or day of the week. Police officers may be on call 24 hours a day; even when they are not on duty, they are usually required by law to respond to emergencies or criminal activity. Although they are assigned regular work hours, individuals in police work must be willing to live by an unpredictable and often erratic work schedule. The work demands constant mental and physical alertness as well as great physical strength and stamina.

Police work generally consists of an eight-hour day and a five-day week, but police officers may work night and weekend shifts and on holidays. Emergencies may add many extra hours to an officer's day or week. The occupation is considered dangerous. Some officers are killed or wounded while performing their duties. Their work can involve unpleasant duties and expose them to sordid, depressing, or dangerous situations. They may be called on to deal with all types of people under many types of circumstances. While the routine of some assigned duties may become boring, the dangers of police work are often stressful for the officers and their families. Police work in general holds the potential for the unknown and unexpected, and most people who pursue this work have a strong passion for and commitment to police work.

Outlook

Employment of police officers is expected to increase faster than the average for all occupations through the year 2008. Federal "tough-on-crime" legislation passed in the mid-1990s has created a short-term increase of new jobs in police departments at the federal, state, and local levels.

The opportunities that become available, however, may be affected by technological, scientific, and other changes occurring today in police work. Automation in traffic control is limiting the number of officers needed in this area, while the increasing reliance on computers throughout society is creating demands for new kinds of police work. New approaches in social science and psychological research are also changing the methodology used in working with public offenders. These trends indicate a future demand for more educated, specialized personnel.

This occupation has a very low turnover rate. However, new positions will open as current officers retire, leave the force, or move into higher positions. Retirement ages are relatively low in police work compared to other occupations. Many officers retire while in their forties and then pursue a second career. In response to increasing crime rates, some police departments across the country are expanding the number of patrol officers; however, budget problems faced by many municipalities may limit growth.

In the past decade, private security firms have begun to take over some police activities such as patrolling airports and other public places. Some private companies have even been contracted to provide police forces for some cities. Many companies and universities also operate their own police forces.

For More Information

The educational arm of the American Federation of Police and the National Association of Chiefs of Police, the American Police Academy compiles statistics, operates a placement service and a speaker's bureau, and offers home study programs. For more information, contact:
American Police Academy
      1000 Connecticut Avenue, NW, Suite 9
      Washington, DC 20036
      Tel: 202-293-9088

The following association maintains a speaker's bureau, conducts educational programs, and offers both recognition and scholarship awards. For more information, contact:

National Police Officers Association of America

PO Box 22129
Louisville, KY 40252-0129
Tel: 800-467-6762

The following organization compiles statistics, operates a hotline, hall of fame, and speaker's bureau, offers children's services, and sponsors competitions and scholarships:

National United Law Enforcement Officers Association

256 East McLemore Avenue
Memphis, TN 38106
Tel: 800-533-4649

Registered Nurses

Overview

Registered nurses *(RNs) help individuals, families, and groups to achieve health and prevent disease. They care for the sick and injured in hospitals and other health care facilities, physicians' offices, private homes, public health agencies, schools, camps, and industry. Some registered nurses are employed in private practice.*

The Job

Registered nurses work under the direct supervision of nursing departments and in collaboration with physicians. Two-thirds of all nurses work in hospitals, where they may be assigned to general, operating room, or maternity room duty. They may also care for sick children or be assigned to other hospital units, such as emergency rooms, intensive care units, or outpatient clinics. There are many different kinds of RNs.

General duty nurses work together with other members of the health care team to assess the patient's condition and to develop and implement a plan of health care. These nurses may perform such tasks as taking patients' vital signs, administering medication and injections, recording the symptoms and progress of patients, changing dressings, assisting patients with personal care, conferring with members of the medical staff, helping prepare a patient for surgery, and completing any number of duties that require skill and understanding of patients' needs.

Surgical nurses oversee the preparation of the operating room and the sterilization of instruments. They assist surgeons during operations and coordinate the flow of patient cases in operating rooms.

Maternity nurses help in the delivery room, take care of newborns in the nursery, and teach mothers how to feed and care for their babies.

The activities of staff nurses are directed and coordinated by *head nurses* and *supervisors.* Heading up the entire nursing program in the hospital is the nursing service director, who administers the nursing program to maintain standards of patient care. The *nursing service director* advises the medical staff, department heads, and the hospital administrator in matters relating to nursing services and helps prepare the department budget.

Private duty nurses may work in hospitals or in a patient's home. They are employed by the patient they are caring for or by the patient's family. Their service is designed for the individual care of one person and is carried out in cooperation with the patient's physician.

Office nurses usually work in the office of a dentist, physician, or health maintenance organization (HMO). They may be one of several nurses on the staff or the only staff nurse. If a nurse is the only staff member, this person may have to combine some clerical duties with those of nursing, such as serving as receptionist, making appointments for the doctor, helping maintain patient records, sending out monthly statements, and attending to routine correspondence. If the physician's staff is a large one that includes secretaries and clerks, the office nurse will concentrate on screening patients, assisting with examinations, supervising the examining rooms, sterilizing equipment, providing patient education, and performing other nursing duties.

Occupational health nurses, or *industrial nurses,* are an important part of many large firms. They maintain a clinic at a plant or factory and are usually occupied in rendering preventive, remedial, and educational nursing services. They work under the direction of an industrial physician, nursing director, or nursing supervisor. They may advise on accident prevention, visit employees on the job to check the conditions under which they work, and advise management about the safety of such conditions. At the plant, they render treatment in emergencies.

School nurses may work in one school or in several, visiting each for a part of the day or week. They may supervise the student clinic, treat minor cuts or injuries, or give advice on good health practices. They may examine students to detect conditions of the eyes or teeth that require attention. They also assist the school physician.

Community health nurses, also called *public health nurses,* require specialized training for their duties. Their job usually requires them to spend part of the time traveling from one assignment to another. Their duties may differ greatly from one case to another. For instance, in one day they may have to instruct a class of expectant mothers, visit new parents to help them plan proper care for the baby, visit an aged patient requiring special care, and conduct a class in nutrition. They usually possess many and varied nursing skills and often are called upon to meet unexpected or unusual situations.

Administrators in the community health field include nursing directors, educational directors, and nursing supervisors. Some nurses go into nursing education and work with nursing students to instruct them on theories and skills they will need to enter the profession. Nursing instructors may give classroom instruction and demonstrations or supervise nursing students on hospital units. Some instructors eventually become nursing school directors, university faculty, or deans of a university degree program. Nurses also have the opportunity to direct staff development and continuing education programs for nursing personnel in hospitals.

Advanced practice nurses are nurses with training beyond that required to have the RN designation. There are four primary categories of nurses included in this category: certified nurse midwives, clinical nurse specialists, nurse anesthetists, and nurse practitioners.

Some nurses are consultants to hospitals, nursing schools, industrial organizations, and public health agencies. They advise clients on such administrative matters as staff organization, nursing techniques, curricula, and education programs. Other administrative specialists include educational directors for the state board of nursing, who are concerned with maintaining well-defined educational standards, and executive directors of professional nurses' associations, who administer programs developed by the board of directors and the members of the association.

Some nurses choose to enter the armed forces. All types of nurses, except private duty nurses, are represented in the military services. They provide skilled nursing care to active-duty and retired members of the armed forces and their families. In addition to basic nursing skills, military nurses are trained to provide care in various environments, including field hospitals, on-air evacuation flights, and onboard ships. Military nurses actively influence the development of health care through nursing research. Advances influenced by military nurses include the development of the artificial kidney (dialysis unit) and the concept of the intensive care unit.

Requirements

High School

High school students interested in becoming a registered nurse should take mathematics and science courses, including biology, chemistry, and physics. English and speech courses should not be neglected because the nurse must be able to communicate well with patients.

Postsecondary Training

There are three basic kinds of training programs that prospective nurses may choose to become registered nurses: associate's degree programs, diploma programs, and bachelor's degree programs. Which of the three training programs to choose depends on one's career goals. A bachelor's degree in nursing is required for most supervisory or administrative positions, for jobs in public health agencies, and for admission to graduate nursing programs. A master's degree is usually necessary to prepare for a nursing specialty or to teach. For some specialties, such as nursing research, a Ph.D. is essential.

The bachelor's degree program is offered by colleges or universities. It requires four (in some cases, five) years to complete. The graduate of this program receives a Bachelor of Science in Nursing degree. The Associate in Arts in Nursing is awarded after completion of a two-year study program that is usually offered in a junior or community college. The student receives hospital training at cooperating hospitals in the general vicinity of the community college. The diploma program, which usually lasts three years, is conducted by hospitals and independent schools. At the conclusion of each of these programs, the student becomes a graduate nurse, but not, however, a registered nurse. To obtain the RN designation the graduate nurse must take and pass a licensing examination required in all states.

In 1998, there were over 2,200 entry-level nursing programs offered in the United States. In addition, there were 198 master's degree and 33 doctoral degree programs. Nurses can pursue postgraduate training that allows them to specialize in certain areas, such as emergency room, operating room, premature nursery, or psychiatric nursing. This training is sometimes offered through hospital on-the-job training programs.

Certification or Licensing

All states and the District of Columbia require a license to practice nursing. To obtain a license, graduates of approved nursing schools must pass a national examination. Nurses may be licensed by more than one state. In some states, continuing education is a condition for license renewal. Different titles require different education and training levels.

Other Requirements

Registered nurses should enjoy working with people, even people who may experiencing fear or anger because of an illness. Patience, compassion, and calmness are qualities needed by anyone practicing this career. In addition, registered nurses must be able to give directions as well as follow instructions and work as part of a health care team. Anyone interested in becoming a registered nurse should also have a strong desire to continue learning, because new tests, procedures, and technologies are constantly being developed for the medical world.

Exploring

High school students can explore their interest in the nursing field in a number of ways. They may read books on careers in nursing and talk with high school guidance counselors, school nurses, and local public health nurses. Visits to hospitals to observe the work and to talk with hospital personnel are also valuable.

Some hospitals now have extensive volunteer service programs in which high school students may work after school, on weekends, or during vacations in order to both render a valuable service and to explore their interests. Other volunteer work experiences may be found with the Red Cross or community health services. Camp counseling jobs sometimes offer related experiences. Some schools offer participation in Future Nurses programs.

Employers

Nurses are employed by hospitals, managed-care facilities, long-term-care facilities, clinics, industry, private homes, schools, camps, and government agencies.

Starting Out

The only way to become a registered nurse is through completion of one of the three kinds of educational programs, plus passing the licensing examination. Registered nurses may apply for employment directly to hospitals, nursing homes, companies, and government agencies that hire nurses. Jobs can also be obtained through school placement offices, by signing up with employment agencies specializing in placement of nursing personnel, or through the state employment office. Other sources of jobs include nurses' associations, professional journals, and newspaper want ads.

Advancement

Increasingly, administrative and supervisory positions in the nursing field go to nurses who have earned at least the bachelor of science degree in nursing. Nurses with many years of experience who are graduates of the diploma program may achieve supervisory positions, but requirements for such promotions have become more difficult in recent years and in many cases require at least the bachelor of science in nursing degree.

Nurses with bachelor's degrees are usually those who are hired as public health nurses. Nurses with master's degrees are often employed as clinical nurse specialists, faculty, instructors, supervisors, or administrators.

RNs can pursue further education to become advanced practice nurses, who have greater responsibilities and command higher salaries.

Earnings

According to the *Occupational Outlook Handbook,* registered nurses earned an average of $40,690 annually in 1998. Fifty percent earned between $34,430 and $49,070. The top 10 percent earned over $69,300 a year.

A Buck Survey found that staff RNs working in a nursing home setting earned an average of about $32,968 a year. Entry-level positions with the Department of Veterans Affairs started at approximately $16,500 for nurses who were graduates of the diploma program or the associate's of arts program. The average annual salary for all nurses in federal government agencies was about $26,100.

Salary is determined by several factors: setting, education, and work experience. Most full-time nurses are given flexible work schedules as well as health and life insurance; some are offered education reimbursement and year-end bonuses. A staff nurse's salary is limited only by the amount of work one is willing to take on. Many nurses take advantage of overtime work and shift differentials. About 10 percent of all nurses hold more than one job.

Work Environment

Most nurses work in facilities that are clean and well lighted and where the temperature is controlled, although some work in rundown inner city hospitals in less than ideal conditions. Usually, nurses work eight-hour shifts. Those in hospitals generally work any of three shifts: 7:00 AM to 3:00 PM; 3:00 PM to 11:00 PM; or 11:00 PM to 7:00 AM.

Nurses spend much of the day on their feet, either walking or standing. Handling patients who are ill or infirm can also be very exhausting. Nurses who come in contact with patients with infectious diseases must be especially careful about cleanliness and sterility. Although many nursing duties are routine, many responsibilities are unpredictable. Sick persons are often very demanding, or they may be depressed or irritable. Despite this, the nurse must retain her or his composure and should be cheerful to help the patient achieve emotional balance.

Community health nurses may be required to visit homes that are in poor condition or very dirty. They may also come in contact with social problems, such as family violence. The nurse is an important health care provider, and in many communities the sole provider.

Both the office nurse and the industrial nurse work regular business hours and are seldom required to work overtime. In some jobs, such as where nurses are on duty in private homes, they may frequently travel from home to home and work with various cases.

Outlook

In 1998, there were about 2.1 million nurses employed in the United States—making this field the largest of all health care occupations. Employment prospects for nurses look good. In fact, it is predicted that there will be about 451,000 additional jobs available through 2008.

Increasing numbers of nurses who have been attracted to the profession in recent years have, however, lessened the demand for nurses in some areas. Even so, there are still many employment opportunities for nurses, especially in the inner cities and in rural areas. Employment opportunities for nurses will be best in home health situations. The increased number of older people and better medical technology have spurred the demand for nurses to bring complicated treatments to the patients' homes.

Employment in nursing homes is expected to grow much faster than the average. Though more people are living well into their 80s and 90s, many need the kind of long term care available at a nursing home. Also, because of financial reasons, patients are being released from hospitals sooner and admitted into nursing homes. Many nursing homes have facilities and staff capable of caring for long term rehabilitation patients, as well as those afflicted with Alzheimer's. Many nurses will also be needed to help staff the growing number of outpatient facilities, such as HMOs, group medical practices, and ambulatory surgery centers.

Two-thirds of all nursing jobs are found in hospitals. However, because of administrative cost cutting, increased nurse's work load, and rapid growth of outpatient services, hospital nursing jobs will experience slower than average growth.

Nursing specialties will be in great demand. There are, in addition, many part-time employment possibilities—approximately 25 percent of all nurses work on a part-time basis.

For More Information

Visit the AACN Web site to access a list of member schools and to read the online pamphlet, Your Nursing Career: A Look at the Facts.
American Association of Colleges of Nursing (AACN)
> 1 Dupont Circle, Suite 530
> Washington, DC 20036
> Tel: 202-463-6930
> Web: http://www.aacn.nche.edu

For information about opportunities as an RN, contact:
American Nurses' Association
> 600 Maryland Avenue, SW, Suite 100W
> Washington, DC 20024-2571
> Tel: 800-274-4ANA
> Web: http://www.nursingworld.org

For information about state-approved programs and information on nursing, contact:
National Association for Practical Nurse Education and Service, Inc.
> 1400 Spring Street, Suite 310
> Silver Spring, MD 20910
> Tel: 301-588-2491
> Email: napnes@aol.com

For general information on nursing, contact:
National League for Nursing
> 61 Broadway
> New York, NY 10006
> Tel: 800-669-1656
> Email: nlnweb@nln.org
> Web: http://www.nln.org/

Secondary School Teachers

Overview

Secondary school teachers *teach students in grades seven through 12. Specializing in one subject area, such as English or math, these teachers work with five or more groups of students during the day. They lecture, direct discussions, and test students' knowledge with exams, essays, and homework assignments.*

The Job

Many successful people credit secondary school teachers with helping guide them into college, careers, and other endeavors. Students may look to secondary school teachers for help in a number of areas. Their primary responsibility to their students in grades seven through 12 is to educate them in a specific subject. But they also inform students about colleges, occupations, and such varied subjects as the arts, health, and relationships. Secondary school teachers may teach in a traditional area, such as science, English, history, and math, or they may teach more specialized classes, such as information technology, business, and theater. Many secondary schools are expanding their course offerings to better serve the individual interests of their students. "School-to-work" programs, which are vocational education programs designed for high school students and recent graduates, involve lab work and demonstrations to prepare students for highly technical jobs. Though they will likely be assigned to one specific level in your subject area, secondary school teachers may be required to teach multiple levels. For example, a secondary school mathematics teacher may teach algebra to a class of ninth-graders one period and trigonometry to high school seniors the next.

In the classroom, secondary school teachers rely on a variety of teaching methods. They spend a great deal of time lecturing, but they also facilitate student discussion and develop projects and activities to interest the students in the subject. They show films and videos, use computers and the Internet, and bring in guest speakers. They assign essays, presentations, and other projects. Each individual subject calls upon particular approaches, and may involve laboratory experiments, role-playing exercises, shop work, and field trips.

Outside of the classroom, secondary school teachers prepare lectures, lesson plans, and exams. They evaluate student work and calculate grades. In the process of planning their class, secondary school teachers read textbooks, novels, and workbooks to determine reading assignments; photocopy notes, articles, and other handouts; and develop grading policies. They also continue to study alternative and traditional teaching methods to hone their skills. They prepare students for special events and conferences and submit student work to competitions. Many secondary school teachers also serve as sponsors to student organizations in their field. For example, a French teacher may sponsor the French club and a journalism teacher may advise the yearbook staff. Some secondary school teachers also have the opportunity for extracurricular work as athletic coaches or drama coaches. Teachers also monitor students during lunch or break times, and sit in on study halls. They may also accompany student groups on field days, and to competitions and events. Some teachers also have the opportunity to escort students on educational vacations to foreign countries, and to Washington, DC, and other major U.S. cities. Secondary school teachers attend faculty meetings, meetings with parents, and state and national teacher conferences.

Some teachers explore their subject area outside of the requirements of the job. English and writing teachers may publish in magazines and journals; business and technology teachers may have small businesses of their own; music teachers may perform and record their music; art teachers may show work in galleries; sign-language teachers may do freelance interpreting.

Requirements

High School

You should follow your guidance counselor's college preparatory program and take advanced classes in such subjects as English, science, math, and government. You should also explore an extracurricular activity, such as theater, sports, and debate, so that you can offer these additional skills to future employers. If you're already aware of which subject you'd like to teach, take all the courses in that area that are available. You should also take speech and composition courses to develop your communication skills.

Postsecondary Training

There are over 500 accredited teacher education programs in the United States. Most of these programs are designed to meet the certification requirements for the state in which they're located. Some states may require that you pass a test before being admitted to an education program. You may choose to major in your subject area while taking required education courses, or you may major in secondary education with a concentration in your subject area. You'll probably have advisors in both colleges to help you select courses. Practice teaching, also called student teaching, in an actual school situation is usually required. The student is placed in a school to work with a full-time teacher. During the period of practice teaching, the undergraduate student will observe the ways in which lessons are presented and the classroom is managed, learn how to keep records of such details as attendance and grades, and get actual experience in handling the class, both under supervision and alone. Besides licensure and courses in education, prospective high school teachers usually need 24 to 36 hours of college work in the subject they wish to teach. Some states require a master's degree; teachers with master's degrees can earn higher salaries. Private schools generally do not require an education degree.

Certification or Licensing

Public school teachers must be licensed under regulations established by the department of education of the state in which they are teaching. Not all states require licensure for teachers in private or parochial schools. When you've received your teaching degree, you may request that a transcript of your college record be sent to the licensure section of the state department of education. If you have met licensure requirements, you will receive a certificate and thus be eligible to teach in the public schools of the state. In some states, you may have to take additional tests. If you move to another state, you will have to resubmit college transcripts, as well as comply with any other regulations in the new state to be able to teach there.

Other Requirements

You'll need respect for young people, and a genuine interest in their success in life. You'll also need patience—adolescence can be a troubling time for children, and these troubles often affect behavior and classroom performance. You'll also be working with students who are at very impressionable ages; you should serve as a good role model. You should also be well organized, as you'll have to keep track of the work and progress of a number of different students.

Exploring

By attending your high school classes, you've already gained a good sense of the daily work of a secondary school teacher. But the requirements of a teacher extend far beyond the classroom, so ask to spend some time with one of your teachers after school, and ask to look at lecture notes and record-keeping procedures. Interview your teachers about the amount of work that goes into preparing a class and directing an extracurricular activity. To get some firsthand teaching experience, volunteer for a peer tutoring program. Many other teaching opportunities may exist in your community—look into coaching an athletic team at the YMCA, counseling at a summer camp, teaching an art course at a community center, or assisting with a community theater production.

Employers

Secondary school teachers are needed at public and private schools, including parochial schools, juvenile detention centers, vocational schools, and schools of the arts. Some Montessori schools are also expanding to include high school courses. Secondary school teachers work in middle schools, junior high schools, and high schools. Though some rural areas maintain schools, most secondary schools are in towns and cities of all sizes. Teachers are also finding opportunities in "charter" schools, which are smaller, deregulated schools that receive public funding.

Starting Out

After completing the teacher certification process, including your months of student teaching, you'll work with your college's placement office to find a full-time position. The departments of education of some states maintain listings of job openings. Many schools advertise teaching positions in the classifieds of the state's major newspapers. You may also directly contact the principals and superintendents of the schools in which you'd like to work. While waiting for full-time work, you can work as a substitute teacher. In urban areas with many schools, you may be able to substitute full-time.

Advancement

Most teachers advance in the sense that they become more expert in the job that they have chosen. There is usually an increase in salary as teachers acquire experience. Additional training or study can also bring an increase in salary.

A few teachers with administrative ability and interest in administrative work may advance to the position of principal. Others may work into supervisory positions, and some may become helping teachers who are charged with the responsibility of helping other teachers find appropriate instructional materials and develop certain phases of their courses of study. Others may go into teacher education at a college or university. For most of these positions, additional education is required. Some teachers also make lateral moves into other education-related positions such as guidance counselor or resource room teacher.

Earnings

Most teachers are contracted to work nine months out of the year, though some contracts are made for 10 or a full 12 months. (When regular school is not in session, teachers are expected to conduct summer teaching, planning, or other school-related work.) In most cases, teachers have the option of prorating their salary up to 52 weeks.

The National Education Association's (NEA) "Rankings of the States, 1997," reported the average annual teacher salary was $38,611. Average salaries ranged from $26,764 in South Dakota to $50,647 in Alaska. The American Federation of Teachers also released survey results in 1997. This report found that the average beginning salary for a teacher with only a bachelor's degree was $25,190. The average maximum salary for a teacher with a master's degree was $44,694.

Teachers can also supplement their earnings through teaching summer classes, coaching sports, sponsoring a club, or other extracurricular work.

On behalf of the teachers, unions bargain with schools over contract conditions such as wages, hours, and benefits. Most teachers join the American Federation of Teachers or the National Education Association. Depending on the state, teachers usually receive a retirement plan, sick leave, and health and life insurance. Some systems grant teachers sabbatical leave.

Work Environment

Although the job of the secondary school teacher is not overly strenuous, it can be tiring and trying. Secondary school teachers must stand for many hours each day, do a lot of talking, show energy and enthusiasm, and handle discipline problems. But they also have the reward of guiding their students as they make decisions about their lives and futures.

Secondary school teachers work under generally pleasant conditions, though some older schools may have poor heating and electrical systems.

Though violence in schools has decreased in recent years, media coverage of the violence has increased, along with student fears. In most schools, students are prepared to learn and to perform the work that's required of them. But in some schools, students may be dealing with gangs, drugs, poverty, and other problems, so the environment can be tense and emotional.

School hours are generally 8 AM to 3 PM, but teachers work more than 40 hours a week teaching, preparing for classes, grading papers, and directing extracurricular activities. As a coach, or as a music or drama director, teachers may have to work some evenings and weekends. Many teachers enroll in master's or doctoral programs and take evening and summer courses to continue their education.

Outlook

The U.S. Department of Education predicts that 322,000 more secondary teachers will be needed by 2008 to meet rising enrollments and to replace the large number of retiring teachers. The NEA believes this will be a challenge because of the low salaries that are paid to secondary school teachers. Higher salaries will be necessary to attract new teachers and retain experienced ones, along with other changes such as smaller classroom sizes and safer schools. Other challenges for the profession involve attracting more men into teaching. The percentage of male teachers at this level continues to decline.

In order to improve education for all children, changes are being considered by some districts. Some private companies are managing public schools. Though it is believed that a private company can afford to provide better facilities, faculty, and equipment, this hasn't been proven. Teacher organizations are concerned about taking school management away from communities and turning it over to remote corporate headquarters. Charter schools and voucher programs are two other controversial alternatives to traditional public education. Charter schools, which are small schools that are publicly funded but not guided by the rules and regulations of traditional public schools, are viewed by some as places of innovation and improved educational methods; others see charter schools as ill-equipped and unfairly funded with money that could better benefit local school districts. Vouchers, which exist only in a few cities, allow students to attend private schools courtesy of tuition vouchers; these vouchers are paid for with public tax dollars. In theory, the vouchers allow for more choices in education for poor and minority students, but private schools still have the option of being highly selective in their admissions.

Teacher organizations see some danger in giving public funds to unregulated private schools.

For More Information

For information about careers, and about the current issues affecting teachers, contact the following organizations, or visit their Web sites.

American Federation of Teachers
> 555 New Jersey Avenue, NW
> Washington, DC 20001
> Tel: 202-879-4400
> Web: http://www.aft.org

National Education Association
> 1201 16th Street, NW
> Washington, DC 20036
> Tel: 202-833-4000
> Web: http://www.nea.org

For information on accredited teacher education programs, contact:
National Council for Accreditation of Teacher Education
> 2010 Massachusetts Avenue, NW, Suite 500
> Washington, DC 20036-1023
> Tel: 202-466-7496
> Email: info@ncate.org
> Web: http://www.ncate.org

Social Workers

Social workers *help people and communities solve problems. These problems include poverty, racism, discrimination, physical and mental illness, addiction, and abuse. They counsel individuals and families, they lead group sessions, they research social problems, and they develop policy and programs. Social workers are dedicated to empowering people and helping people to preserve their dignity and worth.*

The Job

After months of physical abuse from her husband, a young woman has taken her children and moved out of her house. With no job and no home, and fearing for her safety, she looks for a temporary shelter for herself and her children. Once there, she can rely on the help of social workers who will provide her with a room, food, and security. The social workers will offer counseling and emotional support to help her address the problems in her life. They will involve her in group sessions with other victims of abuse. They will direct her to job training programs and other employment services. They will set up interviews with managers of low-income housing. As the woman makes efforts to improve her life, the shelter will provide day care for the children. All these resources exist because the social work profession has long been committed to empowering people and improving society.

The social worker's role extends even beyond the shelter. If the woman has trouble getting help from other agencies, the social worker will serve as an advocate, stepping in to ensure that she gets the aid to which she is entitled. The woman may also qualify for long-term assistance from the shelter, such as a second-step program in which a social worker offers counseling and other support over several months. The woman's individual experience will also help in the social worker's research of the problem of domestic violence; with that research, the social worker can help the community come to a better understanding of the problem and can direct society toward solutions. Some of these solutions may include the development of special police procedures for domestic disputes, or court-ordered therapy groups for abusive spouses.

Direct social work practice is also known as clinical practice. As the name suggests, direct practice involves working directly with the client by offering counseling, advocacy, information and referral, and education. Indirect practice concerns the structures through which the direct practice is offered. Indirect practice (a practice consisting mostly of social workers with Ph.D.s) involves program development and evaluation, administration, and policy analysis. Of the 134,200 members of the National Association of Social Workers (NASW), 69 percent work in direct service roles and 19 percent in indirect roles (according to a recent survey conducted by the NASW).

Because of the number of problems facing individuals, families and communities, social workers find jobs in a variety of settings and with a variety of client groups. Some of these areas are discussed in the following paragraphs:

Health/mental health care. Mental health care has become the lead area of social work employment. These jobs are competitive and typically go to more experienced social workers. Settings include community mental health centers, where social workers serve persistently mentally ill people and participate in outreach services; state and county mental hospitals, for long-term, inpatient care; facilities of the Department of Veterans Affairs, involving a variety of mental health care programs for veterans; and private psychiatric hospitals, for patients who can pay directly. Social workers also work with patients who have physical illnesses. They help individuals and their families adjust to the illness and the changes that illness may bring to their lives. They confer with physicians and with other members of the medical team to make plans about the best way to help the patient. They explain the treatment and its anticipated outcome to both the patient and the family. They help the patient adjust to the possible prospect of long hospitalization and isolation from the family.

Child care/family services. Efforts are being made to offer a more universal system of care that would incorporate child care, family services, and community service. Child care services include day care homes, child care centers, and Head Start centers. Social workers in this setting attempt to address all the problems children face from infancy to late adolescence. They work with families to detect problems early and intervene when necessary. They research the problems confronting children and families, and they establish new services or adapt existing services to address these problems. They provide parenting education to teenage parents, which can involve living with a teenage mother in a foster care situation, teaching parenting skills, and caring for the baby while the mother attends school. Social workers alert employers to employees' needs for daytime child care.

Social workers in this area of service are constantly required to address new issues; in recent years, for example, social workers have developed services for families composed of different cultural backgrounds, services for children with congenital disabilities resulting from the mother's drug use, and disabilities related to HIV or AIDS.

Gerontological social work. Within this field, social workers provide individual and family counseling services in order to assess the older person's needs and strengths. Social workers help older people locate transportation and housing services. They also offer adult day care services, or adult foster care services that match older people with families. Adult protective services protect older people from abuse and neglect, and respite services allow family members time off from the care of an older person. A little-recognized problem is the rising incidence of AIDS among the elderly; 10 percent of all AIDS patients are aged 50 or over.

School social work. In schools, social workers serve students and their families, teachers, administrators, and other school staff members. Education, counseling, and advocacy are important aspects of school social work. With education, social workers attempt to prevent alcohol and drug abuse, teen pregnancy, and the spread of AIDS and other sexually transmitted diseases. They provide multicultural and family life education. They counsel students who are discriminated against because of their sexual orientation or racial, ethnic, or religious background. They also serve as advocates for these students, bringing issues of discrimination before administrators, school boards, and student councils.

A smaller number of social workers are employed in the areas of social work education (a field composed of the professors and instructors who teach and train students of social work); group practice (in which social workers facilitate treatment and support groups); and corrections (providing services to inmates in penal institutions). Social workers also offer counseling, occupational assistance, and advocacy to those with addictions and disabilities, to the homeless, and to women, children, and the elderly who have been in abusive situations.

Client groups expand and change as societal problems change. Social work professionals must remain aware of the problems affecting individuals and communities in order to offer assistance to as many people as possible.

Computers have become important tools for social workers. Client records are maintained on computers, allowing for easier collection and analysis of data. Interactive computer programs are used in training social workers, as well as to analyze case histories (such as for an individual's risk of HIV infection).

Requirements

High School

To prepare for social work, you should take courses in high school that will improve your communications skills, such as English, speech, and composition. On a debate team, you could further develop your skills in communication as well as research and analysis. History, social studies, and sociology courses are important in understanding the concerns and issues of society. Although some work is available for those with only a high school diploma or associate's degree (as a social work aide or social services technician), the most opportunities exist for people with degrees in social work.

Postsecondary Training

The Council on Social Work Education requires that five areas be covered in accredited bachelor's degree social work programs: human behavior and the social environment; social welfare policy and services; social work practice; research; and field practicum. Most programs require two years of liberal arts study followed by two years of study in the social work major. Also, students must complete a field practicum of at least 400 hours. Graduates of these programs can find work in public assistance or they can work with the elderly or with people with mental or developmental disabilities.

Although no clear lines of classification are drawn in the social work profession, most supervisory and administrative positions require at least an MSW. Master's programs are organized according to fields of practice (such as mental health care), problem areas (substance abuse), population groups (the elderly), and practice roles (practice with individuals, families, or communities). They are usually two-year programs, with at least 900 hours of field practice. Most positions in mental health care facilities require an MSW. Doctoral degrees are also available and prepare students for research and teaching. Most social workers with doctorates go to work in community organizations.

Certification or Licensing

Licensing, certification, or registration of social workers is required by all states. To receive the necessary licensing, a social worker will typically have to gain a certain amount of experience and also pass an exam. Five voluntary certification programs help to identify those social workers who have gained the knowledge and experience necessary to meet national standards.

Other Requirements

Social work requires great dedication. As a social worker, you have the responsibility of helping whole families, groups, and communities, as well as focusing on the needs of individuals. Your efforts will not always be supported by the society at large; sometimes you must work against a community's prejudice, disinterest, and denial. You must also remain sensitive to the problems of your clients, offering support, and not moral judgment or personal bias. The only way to effectively address new social problems and new client groups is to remain open to the thoughts and needs of all human beings. Assessing situations and solving problems requires clarity of vision and a genuine concern for the well-being of others.

With this clarity of vision, your work will be all the more rewarding. Social workers have the satisfaction of making a connection with other people and helping them through difficult times. Along with the rewards, however, the work can provide a great deal of stress. Hearing repeatedly about the deeply troubled lives of prison inmates, the mentally ill, abused women and children, and others can be depressing and defeating. Trying to convince society of the need for changes in laws and services can be a long, hard struggle. You must have perseverance to fight for your clients against all odds.

Exploring

As a high school student, you may find openings for summer or part-time work as a receptionist or file clerk with a local social service agency. If there is no opportunity for paid employment, you could work as a volunteer. Good experience is also provided by work as a counselor in a camp for children with physical, mental, or developmental disabilities. Your local YMCA, park district, or other recreational facility may need volunteers for group recreation programs, including programs designed for the prevention of delinquency. By reporting for your high school newspaper, you'll have the opportunity to interview people, conduct surveys, and research social change, all of which are important aspects of the social work profession.

You could also volunteer a few afternoons a week to read to people in retirement homes or to the blind. Work as a tutor in special education programs is sometimes available to high school students.

Employers

Social workers can be employed in direct, or clinical, practice, providing individual and family counseling services, or they may work as administrators for the organizations that provide direct practice. Social workers are employed by community health and mental health centers; hospitals and mental hospitals; child care, family services, and community service organizations, including day care and Head Start programs; elderly care programs, including adult protective services and adult day care and foster care; prisons; shelters and halfway houses; schools; courts; and nursing homes.

Starting Out

Most students of social work pursue a master's degree and in the process learn about the variety of jobs available. They also make valuable connections through faculty and other students. Through the university's job placement service or an internship program, a student will learn about job openings and potential employers.

A social work education in an accredited program will provide you with the most opportunities, and the best salaries and chances for promotion, but practical social work experience can also earn you full-time employment. A part-time job or volunteer work will introduce you to social work professionals who can provide you with career guidance and letters of reference. Agencies with limited funding may not be able to afford to hire social workers with MSWs and will therefore look for applicants with a great deal of experience and lower salary expectations.

Advancement

The attractive and better-paying jobs tend to go to those with more years of practical experience. Dedication to your job, an extensive resume, and good references will lead to advancement in the profession. Also, many social work programs offer continuing education workshops, courses, and seminars. These refresher courses help practicing social workers to refine their skills and to learn about new areas of practice and new methods and problems. The courses are intended to supplement your social work education, not substitute for a bachelor's or master's degree. These continuing education courses can lead to job promotions and salary increases.

Earnings

The higher your degree, the more money you can make in the social work profession. Your area of practice also determines earnings. The areas of mental health, group services, and community organization and planning provide higher salaries, while elderly and disabled care generally provide lower pay. Salaries also vary among regions; social workers on the east and west coasts earn higher salaries than those in the Midwest. Earnings in Canada vary from province to province as well. During the first five years of practice, your salary will increase faster than in later years.

The median salary range for social workers in the United States was approximately $30,590 in 1998, according to the *Occupational Outlook Handbook*. The top 10 percent earned more than $49,080, while the lowest 10 percent earned less than $19,250. Social workers employed by the U.S. government earn an average annual salary of about $45,300. Average salaries in Canada are higher, with a median range of $40,000 to $45,000.

Although women make up a large percentage of the profession, only 2.2 percent of female social workers in the United States receive more than $60,000, as opposed to 6.3 percent of male social workers.

Work Environment

Social workers do not always work at a desk. When they do, they may be interviewing clients, writing reports, or conferring with other staff members. Depending on the size of the agency, office duties such as typing letters, filing, and answering phones may be performed by an aide or volunteer. Social workers employed at shelters or halfway houses may spend most of their time with clients, tutoring, counseling, or leading groups.

Some social workers have to drive to remote areas to make a home visit. They may go into inner city neighborhoods, schools, courts, or jails. In larger cities, domestic violence and homeless shelters are sometimes located in rundown or dangerous areas. Most social workers are involved directly with the people they serve and must carefully examine the client's living conditions and family relations. Although some of these living conditions can be pleasant and demonstrate a good home situation, others can be squalid and depressing.

Advocacy involves work in a variety of different environments. Although much of this work may require making phone calls and sending faxes and letters, it also requires meetings with clients' employers, directors of agencies, local legislators, and others. It may sometimes require testifying in court as well.

Outlook

The field of social work is expected to grow much faster than the average for all occupations through 2008, according to the U.S. Department of Labor. The greatest factor for this growth is the increased number of older people who are in need of social services. Social workers that specialize in gerontology will find many job opportunities in nursing homes, hospitals, and home health care agencies. The needs of the future elderly population are likely to be different from those of the present elderly. Currently, the elderly appreciate community living, while subsequent generations may demand more individual care.

Schools will also need more social workers to deal with issues such as teenage pregnancies, children from single-parent households, and any adjustment problems recent immigrants may have. The trend to integrate students with disabilities into the general school population will require the expertise of social workers to make the transition smoother. However, job availability in schools will depend on funding given by state and local sources.

To help control costs, hospitals are encouraging early discharge for some of their patients. Social workers will be needed by hospitals to help secure health services for patients in their homes. There is also a growing number of people with physical disabilities or impairments staying in their own homes, requiring home health care workers.

Increased availability of health insurance funding and the growing number of people able to pay for professional help will create opportunities for those in private practice. Many businesses hire social workers to help in employee assistance programs, often on a contractual basis.

Poverty is still a main issue addressed by social workers. Families are finding it increasingly challenging to make ends meet on wages that are just barely above the minimum. The problem of fathers who do not make their court-ordered child support payments forces single mothers to work more than one job or rely on welfare. An increased awareness of domestic violence has also pointed up the fact that many of the homeless and unemployed are women who have left abusive situations. Besides all this, working with the poor is often considered unattractive, leaving many social work positions in this area unfilled.

Competition for jobs in urban areas will remain strong. However, there is still a shortage of social workers in rural areas; these areas usually cannot offer the high salaries or modern facilities that attract large numbers of applicants.

The social work profession is constantly changing. The survival of social service agencies, both private and public, depends on shifting political, economic, and workplace issues.

Social work professionals are worried about the threat of declassification. Because of budget constraints and a need for more workers, some agencies have lowered their job requirements. When unable to afford qualified professionals, they hire those with less education and experience. This downgrading raises questions about quality of care and professional standards. Just as in some situations low salaries push out the qualified social worker, so do high salaries. In the area of corrections, attractive salaries (up to $40,000 for someone with a two-year associate's degree) have resulted in more competition from other service workers.

Liability is another growing concern. If a social worker, for example, tries to prove that a child has been beaten or attempts to remove a child from his or her home, the worker can potentially be sued for libel. At the other extreme, a social worker can face criminal charges for failure to remove a child from an abusive home. More social workers are taking out malpractice insurance.

For More Information

For information on social work careers and educational programs, contact:
Council on Social Work Education
1725 Duke Street, Suite 500
Alexandria, VA 22314
Tel: 703-683-8080
Email: info@cswe.org
Web: http://www.cswe.org

Visit the NASW Web site to access the online publication, Choices: Careers in Social Work.
National Association of Social Workers (NASW)
750 First Street, NE, Suite 700
Washington DC 20002-4241
Tel: 202-408-8600
Email: info@naswdc.org
Web: http://www.naswdc.org

For information on educational programs, contact:
Canadian Association of Schools of Social Work
383 Parkdale Avenue, Suite 206
Ottawa, ON K1Y 4R4 Canada
Email: cassw@cassw-acess.ca
Web: http://www.cassw-acess.ca/

Software Designers

Software designers are responsible for creating new ideas and designing prepackaged and customized computer software. Software designers devise applications, such as word processors, front-end database programs, and spreadsheets, that make it possible for computers to complete given tasks and to solve problems. Once a need in the market has been identified, software designers first conceive of the program on a global level by outlining what the program will do. Then they write the specifications from which programmers code computer commands to perform the given functions.

The Job

Without software, computer hardware would have nothing to do. Computers need to be told exactly what to do. Software is the set of codes that gives the computer those instructions. It comes in the form of the familiar prepackaged software that you find in a computer store, such as games, word processing programs, spreadsheets, and desktop publishing programs, and in a customized application designed to fit the specific need of a particular business. Software designers are the initiators of these complex programs. *Computer programmers* then create the software by writing the code that carries out the directives of the designer.

Software designers must envision every detail of what an application will do, how it will do it, and how it will look (the user interface). A simple example is how a home accounting program is created. The software designer first lays out the overall functionality of the program, specifying what it should be able to do, such as balancing a checkbook, keeping track of incoming and outgoing bills, and maintaining records of expenses. For each of these tasks, the software designer will outline the design detail for the specific functions that he or she has mandated, such as what menus and icons will be used, what each screen will look like, and whether there will be help or dialog boxes to assist the user. For example, the designer may specify that the expense record part of the program produce a pie chart that shows the percentage of each household expense in the overall household budget. The designer can specify that the program automatically display the pie chart each time a budget assessment is completed or only after the user clicks on the appropriate icon on the toolbar.

Some software companies specialize in building custom-designed software. This software is highly specialized for specific needs or problems of particular businesses. Some businesses are large enough that they employ in-house software designers who create software applications for their computer systems. A related field is software engineering, which involves writing customized complex software to solve a specific engineering or technical problem of a business or industry.

Whether the designer is working on a mass-market or a custom application, the first step is to define the overall goals for the application. This is typically done in consultation with management if working at a software supply company, or with the client if working on a custom-designed project. Then, the software designer studies the goals and problems of the project. If working on custom-designed software, the designer must also take into consideration the existing computer system of the client. Next, the software designer works on the program strategy and specific design detail that he or she has envisioned. At this point, the designer may need to write a proposal outlining the design and estimating time and cost allocations. Based on this report, management or the client decides if the project should proceed.

Once approval is given, the software designer and the programmers begin working on writing the software program. Typically, the software designer writes the specifications for the program, and the *applications programmers* write the programming codes.

In addition to the design detail duties, a software designer may be responsible for writing a user's manual or at least writing a report for what should be included in the user's manual. After testing and de-bugging the program, the software designer will present it to management or to the client.

Requirements

High School

High school students interested in computer science should take as many computer, math, and science courses as possible since they provide fundamental math and computer knowledge and teach analytical thinking skills. Classes that rely on schematic drawing and flowcharts are also very valuable. English and speech courses help students improve their communications skills, which are very important to software designers who must make formal presentations to management and clients. Also, many technical/vocational schools offer programs in software programming and design. The qualities developed by these classes, plus imagination and an ability to work well under pressure, are key to success in software design.

Postsecondary Training

A bachelor's degree in computer science plus one year's experience with a programming language is required for most software designers.

In the past, the computer industry has tended to be pretty flexible about official credentials; demonstrated computer proficiency and work experience have often been enough to obtain a good position. However, as more people enter the field, competition increases, and job requirements become more stringent. Technical knowledge alone does not suffice in the field of software design. The successful software designer should have at least peripheral knowledge of the field for which he or she intends to design software, such as business, education, or science. An individual with a bachelor's degree in computer science with a minor in business or accounting has an excellent chance for employment in designing business/accounting software, for example. " ... [I]ncreasingly, computer professionals need to be very good in business," says David Weldon, senior editor in charge of *Computerworld*'s Information Technology careers coverage, in the article "Scoring the Best Tech Jobs," by Susan Gregory Thomas, on *U.S. News Online*. "I have a stack of resumes three feet high of rejects, and it's not because these candidates didn't have technical backgrounds," says Andrew Popell, cofounder of Harvest Technology, a software company that develops applications for portfolio managers in the financial industry, in the same article. Another example of this is that those with degrees in education and subsequent teaching experience are much sought after as designers for educational software.

Other Requirements

Software design is project- and detail-oriented, and therefore software designers must be patient and diligent. They must also enjoy problem-solving challenges and be able to work under a deadline with minimal supervision. Software designers should also possess good communications skills for consulting both with management and with clients who will have varying levels of technical expertise.

Software companies are looking for individuals with vision and imagination to help them create new and exciting programs to sell in the ever-competitive software market. Superior technical skills and knowledge combined with motivation, imagination, and exuberance makes an attractive candidate.

Exploring

Spending a day with a working software designer or applications programmer will allow you to experience firsthand what this work entails. School guidance counselors can often help you organize such a meeting.

If you are interested in computer industry careers in general, you should learn as much as possible about computers. You should keep up with new technology by reading computer magazines and by talking to other computer users. You should join computer clubs and use online services and the Internet for information about this field.

Advanced students can put their design/programming knowledge to work by designing and programming their own applications, such as simple games and utility programs.

Employers

Software designers are employed throughout the United States. Opportunities are best in large cities and suburbs where business and industry are active. Programmers who develop software systems work for software manufacturers, many of whom are in Silicon Valley, in northern California. There is also a concentration of software manufacturers in Boston, Chicago, and Atlanta, among other places. Designers who adapt and tailor the software to meet specific needs of end-users work for those end-user companies, many of which are scattered across the country.

Starting Out

Software design positions are regarded as some of the most interesting, and therefore the most competitive, in the computer industry. Some software designers are promoted from an entry-level programming position. Software design positions in software supply companies and large custom software companies will be difficult to secure straight out of college or technical/vocational school.

Entry-level programming and design jobs may be listed in the help wanted sections of newspapers. Employment agencies and online job banks are other good sources.

Students in technical schools or universities should take advantage of the campus placement office. They should check regularly for internship postings, job listings, and notices of on-campus recruitment. Placement offices are also valuable resources for resume tips and interviewing techniques. Internships and summer jobs with such corporations are always beneficial and provide experience that will give you the edge over your competition. General computer job fairs are also held throughout the year in larger cities.

There are many online career sites listed on the World Wide Web that post job openings, salary surveys, and current employment trends. The Web also has online publications that deal specifically with computer jobs. Interested students can obtain information from computer organizations such as the IEEE Computer Society. Because this is such a competitive field, applicants will need to show initiative and creativity that will set themselves apart from other applicants.

Advancement

In general, programmers work between one and five years before being promoted to software designer. A programmer can move up by demonstrating an ability to create new software ideas that translate well into marketable applications. Individuals with a knack for spotting trends in the software market are also likely to advance.

Those software designers who demonstrate leadership may be promoted to project team leader. Project team leaders are responsible for developing new software projects and overseeing the work done by software designers and applications programmers. With experience as a project team leader, a motivated software designer may be promoted to a position as a software manager who runs projects from an even higher level.

The key to advancement in software design is keeping up-to-date with changing technology. A career in the computer industry means that education never stops. For advancement as a software designer, it means not only keeping up with advances in computer technology, it means making the changes happen.

Earnings

Salaries for software designers vary with the size of the company and with location. Salaries may be slightly higher in areas where there is a large concentration of computer companies, such as the Silicon Valley in northern California and parts of Washington, Oregon, and the East Coast.

Starting salaries for software designers range from $50,000 to $65,000, according to the *Occupational Outlook Handbook*. Senior designer or project team leaders can earn as much as $80,000 a year. At the managerial level, salaries are even higher and can reach $100,000+.

Most designers work for large companies, which offer a full benefits package that includes health insurance, vacation and sick time, and a profit sharing or retirement plan.

Work Environment

Software designers work in comfortable environments. Many computer companies are known for their casual work atmosphere; employees generally do not have to wear suits, except during client meetings. Overall, software designers work standard weeks. However, they may be required to work overtime near a deadline. It is common in software design to share office or cubical space with two or three coworkers, which is typical of the team approach to working. As a software designer or applications programmer, much of the day is spent in front of the computer, although a software designer will have occasional team meetings or meetings with clients.

Software design can be stressful work for several reasons. First, the market for software is very competitive and companies are pushing to develop more innovative software and to get it on the market before the competitors. For this same reason, software design is also very exciting and creative work. Second, software designers are given a project and a deadline. It is up to the designer and team members to budget their time to finish in the allocated time. Finally, working with programming languages and so many details can be very frustrating, especially when the tiniest glitch means the program will not run. For this reason, software designers must be patient and diligent.

Outlook

Jobs in software design are expected to grow faster than the average through the year 2008, according to the *Occupational Outlook Handbook*. Employment of computing professionals will grow as technology becomes more sophisticated and organizations continue to adopt and integrate these technologies, making for plentiful job openings. Hardware designers and systems programmers are constantly developing faster, more powerful, and more user-friendly hardware and operating systems. As long as these advancements continue, the industry will need software designers to create software to use these improvements.

Growth rates for the packaged software industry have been extremely vigorous through the 1990s, with an average growth rate of 12 percent per year. Experts are projecting an approximate 10 percent annual growth for software.

Business may have less need to contract for custom software as more prepackaged software arrives on the market that allows users with minimal computer skills to "build" their own software using components that they customize themselves. However, the growth in the retail software market is expected to make up for this loss in customized services.

The expanding integration of Internet technologies by businesses has resulted in a rising demand for a variety of skilled professionals who can develop and support a variety of Internet applications.

For More Information

Contact ACM for information on internships, student membership, and the ACM student magazine, Crossroads. *ACM also offers a student Web site at http://www.acm.org/membership/student/.*
Association for Computing Machinery (ACM)
> 1515 Broadway
> New York, NY 10036-5701
> Tel: 212-869-7440
> Email: SIGS@acm.org
> Web: http://www.acm.org

For information on scholarships, student membership, and the student newsletter, looking.forward, *contact:*
IEEE Computer Society
> 1730 Massachusetts Avenue, NW
> Washington, DC 20036
> Tel: 202-371-0101
> Web: http://www.computer.org

Software Engineers

Overview

Software engineers *are responsible for customizing existing software programs to meet the needs and desires of a particular business or industry. First, they spend considerable time researching, defining, and analyzing the problem at hand. Then, they develop software programs to resolve the problem on the computer.*

The Job

Every day, businesses, scientists, and government agencies encounter difficult problems that they cannot solve manually, either because the problem is just too complicated or because it would take too much time to calculate the appropriate solutions. For example, astronomers receive thousands of pieces of data every hour from probes and satellites in space as well as telescopes here on earth. If they had to process the information themselves; that is, compile careful comparisons with previous years' readings, look for patterns or cycles, and keep accurate records of the origin of the various data, it would be so cumbersome and lengthy a project as to make it next to impossible. They can, however, process the data, but only thanks to the extensive help of computers. Computer software engineers define and analyze specific problems in business or science and help develop computer software applications that effectively solve them. The software engineers that work in the field of astronomy are well versed in its concepts, but many other kinds of software engineers exist as well.

The basic structure of computer engineering is the same in any industry. First, software engineers research specific problems and investigate ways in which computers can be programmed to perform certain functions. Then, they develop software applications customized to the needs and desires of the business or organization. For example, many software engineers work with the federal government and insurance companies to develop new ways of reducing paperwork, such as income tax returns, claims forms, and applications. There are currently several independent but major form automation projects taking place throughout the United States. As software engineers find new ways to solve the problems associated with form automation, more and more forms are completed online and less on paper.

Software engineers specializing in a particular industry, such as a particular science, business, or medicine, are expected to demonstrate a certain level of proficiency in that industry. Consequently, the specific nature of their work varies from project to project and industry to industry. Software engineers also differ by the nature of their employer. Some work for consulting firms, who complete software projects for different clients on an individual basis. Others work for large companies that hire engineers full time to develop software customized to their needs. Software engineering professionals also differ by level of responsibility. *Software engineering technicians* assist engineers in completing projects. They are usually knowledgeable in analog, digital, and microprocessor electronics and programming techniques. Technicians know enough about program design and computer languages to fill in details left out by engineers or programmers, who conceive of the program from a large-scale perspective. Technicians might also test new software applications with special diagnostic equipment.

Software engineering is extremely detail-oriented work. Since computers do only what they are programmed to do, engineers have to account for every bit of information with a programming command. Software engineers are thus required to be very well organized and precise. In order to achieve this, they generally follow strict procedures in completing an assignment.

First, they interview clients and colleagues in order to determine exactly what they want the final program to be able to do. Defining the problem by outlining the goal can sometimes be difficult, especially when clients have little technical training. Then, they evaluate the software applications already in use by the client to understand how and why they are failing to fulfill the needs of the operation. After this period of fact-gathering, the engineers use methods of scientific analysis and mathematical models to develop possible solutions to the problems. These analytical methods allow them to predict and measure the outcomes of different proposed designs.

When they have developed a good notion of what type of program is required to fulfill the client's needs, they draw up a detailed proposal which includes estimates of time and cost allocations. Management must then decide if the project will meet their needs, is a good investment, and whether or not it will be undertaken.

Once a proposal is accepted, both software engineers and technicians begin work on the project. They verify with hardware engineers that the proposed software program is completed with existing hardware systems. Typically, the engineer writes program specifications and the technician uses his or her knowledge of computer languages to write preliminary programming. Engineers focus most of their effort on program strategies, testing procedures, and reviewing technicians' work.

Software engineers are usually responsible for a significant amount of technical writing, including projects proposals, progress reports, and user manuals. They are required to meet regularly with the clients in order to keep project goals clear and learn about any changes as quickly as possible.

When the program is completed, the software engineer organizes a demonstration of the final product to the client. Supervisors, management, and users are generally present. Some software engineers may offer to install the program, train users on it, and make arrangements for ongoing technical support.

Requirements

A high school diploma is the minimum requirement for software engineering technicians. A bachelor's or advanced degree in computer science or engineering is required for most software engineers.

High School

High school students interested in pursuing this career should take as many computer, math, and science courses as possible, since they provide fundamental math and computer knowledge and teach analytical thinking skills. Classes that rely on schematic drawing and flowcharts are also very valuable. English and speech courses help students improve their communications skills, which is very important for software engineers.

Postsecondary Training

There are several ways to enter the field of software engineering, although it is becoming increasingly necessary to pursue formal postsecondary education. Individuals without an associate's degree may first be hired in the quality assurance or technical support departments of a company. Many complete associate degrees while working and then are promoted into software engineering technician positions. As more and more well-educated professionals enter the industry, however, it is becoming more important for applicants to have at least an associate's degree in computer engineering or programming. Many technical and vocational schools offer a variety of programs that prepare students for jobs as software engineering technicians.

Interested students should consider carefully their long-range goals. Being promoted from a technician's job to that of software engineer often requires a bachelor's degree. In the past, the computer industry has tended to be fairly flexible about official credentials; demonstrated computer proficiency and work experience has often been enough to obtain a good position. This may hold true for some in the future. The majority of young computer professionals entering the field for the first time, however, will be college educated. Therefore, those with no formal education or work experience will have less chance of employment.

Obtaining a postsecondary degree in computer engineering is usually considered challenging and even difficult. In addition to natural ability, students should be hard working and determined to succeed. Software engineers planning to work in specific technical fields, such as medicine, law, or business, should receive some formal training in that particular discipline.

Certification or Licensing

Another option for individuals interested in software engineering is to pursue commercial certification. These programs are usually run by computer companies that wish to train professionals in working with their products. Classes are challenging and examinations can be rigorous. New programs are introduced every year.

Other Requirements

Software engineers need strong communications skills in order to be able to make formal business presentations and interact with people having different levels of computer expertise. They must also be detail oriented and work well under pressure.

Exploring

Interested high school students should try to spend a day with a working software engineer or technician in order to experience firsthand what a typical day is like. School guidance counselors can help you arrange such a visit. You may also talk to your high school computer teacher for more information.

In general, you should be intent on learning as much as possible about computers and computer software. You should learn about new developments by reading trade magazines and talking to other computer users.

You also can join computer clubs and surf the Internet for information about working in this field.

Employers

Software engineering is done in many fields, including medical, industrial, military, communications, aerospace, scientific, and other commercial businesses. The majority of software engineers, though, are employed by computer and data processing companies and by consulting firms.

Starting Out

Individuals with work experience and perhaps even an associate's degree are sometimes promoted to software engineering technician positions from entry-level jobs in quality assurance or technical support. Those already employed by computer companies or large corporations should read company job postings to learn about promotion opportunities. Employees who would like to train in software engineering, either on the job or through formal education, can investigate future career possibilities within the same company and advise management of their wish to change career tracks. Some companies offer tuition reimbursement for employees who train in areas applicable to business operations.

Technical, vocational, and university students of software engineering should work closely with their schools' placement offices, as many professionals find their first position through on-campus recruiting. Placement office staff are well trained to provide tips on resume writing and interviewing techniques, and locating job leads.

Individuals not working with a school placement office can check the classified ads for job openings. They also can work with a local employment agency that places computer professionals in appropriate jobs. Many openings in the computer industry are publicized by word of mouth, so interested individuals should stay in touch with working computer professionals to learn who is hiring. In addition, these people may be willing to refer interested job seekers directly to the person in charge of recruiting.

Advancement

With additional education and work experience, software engineering technicians may be promoted to software engineer. Software engineers who demonstrate leadership qualities and thorough technical know-how may become *project team leaders* who are responsible for full-scale software development projects. Project team leaders oversee the work of technicians and engineers. They determine the overall parameters of a project, calculate time schedules and financial budgets, divide the project into smaller tasks, and assign these tasks to engineers. Overall, they do both managerial and technical work.

Software engineers with experience as project team leaders may be promoted to a position as software manager, running a large research and development department. Managers oversee software projects with a more encompassing perspective; they help choose projects to be undertaken, select project team leaders and engineering teams, and assign individual projects. In some cases, they may be required to travel, solicit new business, and contribute to the general marketing strategy of the company.

Many computer professionals find that their interests change over time. As long as individuals are well qualified and keep up-to-date with the latest technology, they are usually able to find positions in other areas within the computer industry.

Earnings

Software engineering technicians usually earn beginning salaries of $24,000. Computer engineers with a bachelor's degree in computer engineering earned starting salaries of $45,700 in 1999, according to the National Association of Colleges and Employers. New computer engineers with a master's degree averaged $58,700. Computer engineers earned median annual salaries of $61,910 in 1998, according to the U.S. Department of Labor. The lowest 10 percent averaged less than $37,150; the highest 10 percent earned $92,850 or more annually. Experienced software engineers can earn over $100,000 a year. When they are promoted into management, as project team leaders or software managers, they earn even more. Software engineers generally earn more in geographical areas where there are clusters of computer companies, such as the Silicon Valley in northern California.

Most software engineers work for companies that offer extensive benefits, including health insurance, sick leave, and paid vacation. In some smaller computer companies, however, benefits may be limited.

Work Environment

Software engineers usually work in comfortable office environments. Overall, they usually work 40-hour weeks, but this depends on the nature of the employer and expertise of the engineer. In consulting firms, for example, it is typical for engineers to work long hours and frequently travel to out-of-town assignments.

Software engineers generally receive an assignment and a time frame within which to accomplish it; daily work details are often left up to the individuals. Some engineers work relatively lightly at the beginning of a project, but work a lot of overtime at the end in order to catch up. Most engineers are not compensated for overtime. Software engineering can be stressful, especially when working to meet deadlines. Working with programming languages and intense details is often frustrating. Therefore, software engineers should be patient, enjoy problem-solving challenges, and work well under pressure.

Outlook

The field of software engineering is expected to be one of the fastest growing occupations through the year 2008, according to the U.S. Department of Labor. Demands made on computers increase every day and from all industries. The development of one kind of software sparks ideas for many others. In addition, users rely on software programs that are increasingly user-friendly.

Since technology changes so rapidly, software engineers are advised to keep up on the latest developments. While the need for software engineers will remain high, computer languages will probably change every few years and software engineers will need to attend seminars and workshops to learn new computer languages and software design. They also should read trade magazines, surf the Internet, and talk with colleagues about the field. These kinds of continuing education techniques help ensure that software engineers are best equipped to meet the needs of the workplace.

For More Information

For more information on careers in computer software, contact:
Software & Information Industry Association
    1730 M Street, NW, Suite 700
    Washington, DC 20036-4510
    Tel: 202-452-1600
    Web: http://www.siia.net

For certification information, contact:
Institute for Certification of Computing Professionals
    2200 East Devon Avenue, Suite 247
    Des Plaines, IL 60018-4503
    Tel: 847-299-4227
    Web: http://www.iccp.org

Contact ACM for information on internships, student membership, and the ACM student magazine, Crossroads. *ACM also offers a student Web site at http://www.acm.org/membership/student/.*

Association for Computing Machinery (ACM)
> One Astor Plaza
> 1515 Broadway
> New York, NY 10036
> Tel: 800-342-6626
> Email: ACMHELP@acm.org
> Web: http://www.acm.org

For information on scholarships, student membership, and the student newsletter, looking.forward, *contact:*

IEEE Computer Society
> 1730 Massachusetts Avenue, NW
> Washington, DC 20036-1992
> Tel: 202-371-0101
> Web: http://www.computer.org

Special Education Teachers

Overview

Special education teachers teach students, aged three through 21, with a variety of disabilities. They design individualized education plans and work with students one-on-one to help them learn academic subjects and life skills.

The Job

Special education teachers instruct students who have a variety of disabilities. Their students may have physical disabilities, such as vision, hearing, or orthopedic impairment. They may also have learning disabilities or serious emotional disturbances. Although less common, special education teachers sometimes work with students who are gifted and talented, children who have limited proficiency in English, children who have communicable diseases, or children who are neglected and abused.

In order to teach special education students, these teachers design and modify instruction so that it is tailored to individual student needs. Teachers collaborate with school psychologists, social workers, parents, and occupational, physical, and speech-language therapists to develop a specially-designed program called an Individualized Education Program (IEP) for each one of their students. The IEP sets personalized goals for a student, based upon his or her learning style and ability, and outlines specific steps to prepare him or her for employment or postsecondary schooling.

Special education teachers teach at a pace that is dictated by the individual needs and abilities of their students. Unlike most regular classes, special education classes do not have an established curriculum that is taught to all students at the same time. Because student abilities vary widely, instruction is individualized and it is part of the teacher's responsibility to match specific techniques with a student's learning style and abilities. They may spend much time working with students one-on-one or in small groups.

Working with different types of students requires a variety of teaching methods. Some students may need to use special equipment or skills in the classroom in order to overcome their disabilities. For example, a teacher working with a student with a physical disability might use a computer that is operated by touching a screen or by voice commands. To work with hearing-impaired students, the teacher may need to use sign language. With visually impaired students, he or she may use teaching materials that have Braille characters or large, easy-to-see type. Gifted and talented students may need extra challenging assignments, a faster learning pace, or special attention in one curriculum area, such as art or music.

In addition to teaching academic subjects, special education teachers help students develop both emotionally and socially. They work to make students as independent as possible by teaching them functional skills for daily living. They may help young children learn basic grooming, hygiene, and table manners. Older students might be taught how to balance a checkbook, follow a recipe, or use the public transportation system.

Special education teachers meet regularly with their students' parents to inform them of their child's progress and offer suggestions of how to promote learning at home. They may also meet with school administrators, social workers, psychologists, various types of therapists, and students' general education teachers.

The current trend in education is to integrate students with disabilities into regular classrooms to the extent that it is possible and beneficial to them. This is often called "mainstreaming." As mainstreaming becomes increasingly common, special education teachers frequently work with general education teachers in general education classrooms. They may help adapt curriculum materials and teaching techniques to meet the needs of students with disabilities and offer guidance on dealing with students' emotional and behavioral problems.

In addition to working with students, special education teachers are responsible for a certain amount of paperwork. They document each student's progress and may fill out any forms that are required by the school system or the government.

Requirements

High School

High school students who are considering a career as a special education teacher should focus on courses that will prepare them for college. These classes include natural and social sciences, mathematics, and English. Speech classes would also be a good choice for improving one's communication skills. Finally, classes in psychology might be helpful both to help prospective teachers understand the students they will eventually teach, and prepare them for college-level psychology course work.

Postsecondary Training

All states require that teachers have at least a bachelor's degree and that they complete a prescribed number of subject and education credits. It is increasingly common for special education teachers to complete an additional fifth year of training after they receive their bachelor's degree. Many states require special education teachers to get a master's degree in special education.

There are approximately 700 colleges and universities in the United States that offer programs in special education, including undergraduate, master's and doctoral programs. These programs include general and specialized courses in special education, including educational psychology, legal issues of special education, child growth and development, and knowledge and skills needed for teaching students with disabilities. The student typically spends the last year of the program student-teaching in an actual classroom, under the supervision of a licensed teacher.

Certification or Licensing

All states also require that special education teachers be licensed, although the particulars of licensing vary by state. In some states, these teachers must first be certified as elementary or secondary school teachers, then meet specific requirements to teach special education. Some states offer general special education licensure; others license several different subspecialties within special education. Some states allow special education teachers to transfer their license from one state to another, but many still require these teachers to pass licensing requirements for that state.

Other Requirements

Special education teachers need to have many of the same personal characteristics as regular classroom teachers: the ability to communicate, a broad knowledge of the arts, sciences, and history, and a love of children. In addition, these teachers need a great deal of patience and persistence. They need to be creative, flexible, cooperative, and accepting of differences in others. Finally, they need to be emotionally stable and consistent in their dealings with students.

Exploring

There are a number of ways for the interested high school student to explore the field of special education. One of the first and easiest might be to approach a special education teacher at his or her school and ask to talk about the job. Perhaps the teacher could provide a tour of the special education classroom, or allow the student to visit while a class is in session.

Students might also become acquainted with special-needs students at their school, or become involved in a school or community mentoring program for these students. There may also be other opportunities for volunteer work or part-time jobs in the school, community agencies, camps, or residential facilities that allow students to work with persons with disabilities.

Employers

The majority of special education teachers work in public school systems. The next largest group are employed by local education agencies, and a minority of others work in colleges and universities, private schools, and state education agencies.

Starting Out

Because public school systems are by far the largest employers of special education teachers, this is where the beginning teacher should focus his or her job search.

Since the special education teacher must have at least a bachelor's degree, he or she should have access to his or her college's career placement center. This may prove a very effective place to begin. The student may also write to the state department of education for information on placement and regulations, or contact state employment offices to enquire about job openings. Applying directly to local school systems can sometimes be effective. Even if a school system does not have an immediate opening, it will usually keep applicant resumes on file, should a vacancy occur.

Advancement

Advancement opportunities for special education teachers, as for regular classroom teachers, are fairly limited. They may take the form of higher wages, better facilities, or more prestige. In some cases, these teachers do advance to become supervisors or administrators, although this may require continued education on the teacher's part. Another option is for special education teachers to earn advanced degrees and become instructors at the college level.

Earnings

In some school districts, salaries for special education teachers follow the same scale as general education teachers. According to the National Education Association, the average salary for special education teachers in 1998 was $37,850, according to the *Occupational Outlook Handbook*. The lowest 10 percent earned less than $25,450, while the highest 10 percent earned more than $78,030. Public secondary schools paid an average of $39,000; elementary schools, $38,000. Private school teachers usually earn less as compared with their public school counterparts. Teachers can supplement their annual salaries by becoming an activity sponsor, or by summer work.

Other school districts pay their special education teachers on a separate scale, which is usually higher than that of general education teachers.

Regardless of the salary scale, special education teachers usually receive a complete benefits package, which includes health and life insurance, paid holidays and vacations, and a pension plan.

Work Environment

The special education teacher usually works from 7:30 or 8:00 AM to 3:00 or 3:30 PM. Like most teachers, however, he or she typically spends several hours in the evening grading papers, completing paperwork, or preparing lessons for the next day. Altogether, most special education teachers work more than the standard 40 hours per week.

Although some schools offer year-round classes for students, the majority of special education teachers work the traditional 10-month school year, with a two-month vacation in the summer. Many teachers find this work schedule very appealing, as it gives them the opportunity to pursue personal interests or additional education during the summer break. Teachers typically also get a week off at Christmas and for spring break.

Special education teachers work in a variety of settings in schools, including both ordinary and specially equipped classrooms, resource rooms, and therapy rooms. Some schools have newer and better facilities for special education than others. Although it is less common, some teachers work in residential facilities or tutor students who are homebound or hospitalized.

Working with special education students can be very demanding, due to their physical and emotional needs. Teachers may fight a constant battle to keep certain students, particularly those with behavior disorders, under control. Other students, such as those with mental impairments or learning disabilities, learn so slowly that it may seem as if they are making no progress. The special education teacher must deal daily with frustration, setbacks, and classroom disturbances.

These teachers must also contend with heavy workloads, including a great deal of paperwork to document each student's progress. In addition, they may sometimes be faced with irate parents who feel that their child is not receiving proper treatment or an adequate education.

The positive side of this job is in helping students overcome their disabilities and learn to be as functional as possible. For a special education teacher, knowing that he or she is making a difference in a child's life can be very rewarding and emotionally fulfilling.

Outlook

The field of special education is expected to grow faster than the average through the year 2008, according to the U.S. Department of Labor. This demand is caused partly by the growth in the number of special education students needing services. Medical advances resulting in more survivors of illness and accidents, the rise in birth defects, especially in older pregnancies, as well as general population growth, are also significant factors for strong demand. Because of the rise in the number of youths with disabilities under the age of 21, the government has given approval for more federally funded programs. Growth of jobs in this field has also been influenced positively by legislation emphasizing training and employment for individuals with disabilities and a growing public awareness and interest in those with disabilities.

Finally, there is a fairly high turnover rate in this field, as special education teachers find the work too stressful and switch to mainstream teaching or change jobs altogether. Many job openings will arise out of a need to replace teachers who have left their positions. There is a shortage of qualified teachers in rural areas and in the inner city. Jobs will also be plentiful for teachers who specialize in speech and language impairments, learning disabilities, and early childhood intervention. Bilingual teachers with multicultural experience will be in high demand.

For More Information

Council of Administrators of Special Education
615 16th Street, NW
Albuquerque, NM 87104
Tel: 505-243-7622
Email: thomason@apsicc.aps.edu

For information on accredited schools, teacher certification, financial aid, and careers in special education, contact:

National Clearinghouse for Professions in Special Education, Council for Exceptional Children
>   1920 Association Drive
>   Reston, VA 20191-1589
>   Tel: 800-328-0272
>   Web: http://www.special-ed-careers.org

Technical Support Specialists

Overview

Technical support specialists investigate and resolve problems in computer functioning. They listen to customer complaints, walk customers through possible solutions, and write technical reports based on these events. Technical support specialists have different duties depending on whom they assist and what they fix. Regardless of specialty, all technical support specialists must be very knowledgeable about the products with which they work and be able to communicate effectively with users from different technical backgrounds. They must be patient with frustrated users and be able to perform well under stress. Technical support is basically like solving mysteries, so support specialists should enjoy the challenge of problem solving and have strong analytical thinking skills.

The Job

It is relatively rare today to find a business that does not rely on computers for at least something. Some use them heavily and in many areas: daily operations, like employee time clocks; monthly projects, like payroll and sales accounting; and major reengineering of fundamental business procedures, like form automation in government agencies, insurance companies, and banks. Once employees get used to performing their work on computers, they soon can barely remember how they ever got along without them. As more companies become increasingly reliant on computers, it becomes increasingly critical that they function properly all the time. Any computer downtime can be extremely expensive, in terms of work left undone and sales not made, for example. When employees experience problems with their computer system, they call technical support for help. Technical support specialists investigate and resolve problems in computer functioning.

Technical support can generally be broken up into at least three distinct areas, although these distinctions vary greatly with the nature, size, and scope of the company. The three most prevalent areas are user support, technical support, and microcomputer support. Most technical support specialists perform some combination of the tasks explained below.

The jobs of technical support specialists vary according to whom they assist and what they fix. Some specialists help private users exclusively; others are on call to a major corporate buyer. Some work with computer hardware and software, while others help with printer, modem, and fax problems. *User support specialists,* also known as *help desk specialists,* work directly with users themselves, who call when they experience problems. The support specialist listens carefully to the user's explanation of the precise nature of the problem and the commands entered that seem to have caused it. Some companies have developed complex software that allows the support specialist to enter a description of the problem and wait for the computer to provide suggestions about what the user should do.

The initial goal is to isolate the source of the problem. If user error is the culprit, the technical support specialist explains procedures related to the program in question, whether it is a graphics, database, word processing, or printing program. If the problem seems to lie in the hardware or software, the specialist asks the user to enter certain commands in order to see if the computer makes the appropriate response. If it does not, the support specialist is closer to isolating the cause. The support specialist consults supervisors, programmers, and others in order to outline the cause and possible solutions.

Some technical support specialists who work for computer companies are mainly involved with solving problems whose cause has been determined to lie in the computer system's operating system, hardware, or software. They make exhaustive use of resources, such as colleagues or books, and try to solve the problem through a variety of methods, including program modifications and the replacement of certain hardware or software.

Technical support specialists employed in the information systems departments of large corporations do this kind of troubleshooting as well. They also oversee the daily operations of the various computer systems in the company. Sometimes they compare the system's work capacity to the actual daily workload in order to determine if upgrades are needed. In addition, they might help out other computer professionals in the company with modifying commercial software for their company's particular needs.

Microcomputer support specialists are responsible for preparing computers for delivery to a client, including installing the operating system and desired software. After the unit is installed at the customer's location, the support specialists might help train users on appropriate procedures and answer any questions they have. They help diagnose problems as they arise, transferring major concerns to other technical support specialists.

All technical support work must be well documented. Support specialists write detailed technical reports on every problem they work on. They try to tie together different problems on the same software, so programmers can make adjustments that address all of them. Record keeping is crucial because designers, programmers, and engineers use technical support reports to revise current products and improve future ones. Some support specialists help write training manuals. They are often required to read trade magazines and company newsletters in order to keep up-to-date on their products and the field in general.

Requirements

High School

A high school diploma is a minimum requirement for technical support specialists. Any technical courses you can take—like computer science, schematic drawing, or electronics—can help you develop the logical and analytical thinking skills necessary to be successful in this field. Courses in math and science are also valuable for this reason. Since technical support specialists have to deal with both computer programmers on the one hand and computer users who may not know anything about computers on the other, you should take English and speech classes to improve your communications skills, both verbal and written.

Postsecondary Training

Technical support is a field as old as computer technology itself, so it might seem odd that postsecondary programs in this field are not more common or standardized. The reason behind this situation is relatively simple—formal education curricula cannot keep up with the changes, nor can they provide specific training on individual products. Some large corporations might consider educational background, both as a way to weed out applicants and to insure a certain level of proficiency. Most major computer companies, however, look for energetic individuals who demonstrate a willingness and ability to learn new things quickly and who have general computer knowledge. These employers count on training new support specialists themselves.

Individuals interested in pursuing a job in this field should first determine what area of technical support appeals to them the most and then honestly assess their level of experience and knowledge. Large corporations often prefer to hire people with an associate's degree and some experience. They may also be impressed with commercial certification in a computer field, like networking. However, if they are hiring from within the company, they will probably weigh experience more heavily than education when making a final decision.

Employed individuals looking for a career change may want to commit themselves to a program of self-study in order to be qualified for technical support positions. Many computer professionals learn a lot of what they know by playing around on computers, reading trade magazines, and talking with computer professionals. Self-taught individuals should learn how to effectively demonstrate knowledge and proficiency on the job or during an interview. Besides self-training, employed individuals should investigate the tuition reimbursement programs offered by their company.

High school students with no experience should seriously consider earning an associate's degree in a computer-related technology. The degree shows the prospective employer that the applicant has attained a certain level of proficiency with computers and has the intellectual ability to learn technical processes, a promising sign for success on the job.

There are many computer technology programs that lead to an associate's degree. A specialization in PC support and administration is certainly applicable to technical support. Most computer professionals eventually need to go back to school to earn a bachelor's degree in order to keep themselves competitive in the job market and prepare themselves for promotion to other computer fields.

Other Requirements

Technical support specialists should be patient, enjoy challenges of problem solving, and think logically. They should work well under stress and demonstrate effective communication skills. Working in a field that changes rapidly, they should be naturally curious and enthusiastic about learning new technologies as they are developed.

Exploring

If you are interested in becoming a technical support specialist, you should try to organize a career day with an employed technical support specialist. Local computer repair shops that offer technical support service might be a good place to look. Otherwise, you should contact major corporations, computer companies, and even the central office of your school system.

If you are interested in any computer field, you should start working and playing on computers as much as possible; many working computer professionals became computer hobbyists at a very young age. You can surf the Internet, read computer magazines, and join school or community computer clubs.

You might also attend a computer technology course at a local technical/vocational school. This would give you hands-on exposure to typical technical support training. In addition, if you experience problems with your own hardware or software, you should call technical support, paying close attention to how the support specialist handles the call and asking as many questions as the specialist has time to answer.

Employers

Technical support specialists work for computer hardware and software companies, as well as in the information systems departments of large corporations and government agencies.

Starting Out

Most technical support positions are considered entry-level. They are found mainly in computer companies and large corporations. Individuals interested in obtaining a job in this field should scan the classified ads for openings in local businesses and may want to work with an employment agency for help finding out about opportunities. Since many job openings are publicized by word of mouth, it is also very important to speak with as many working computer professionals as possible. They tend to be aware of job openings before anyone else and may be able to offer a recommendation to the hiring committee.

If students of computer technology are seeking a position in technical support, they should work closely with their school's placement office. Many employers inform placement offices at nearby schools of openings before ads are run in the newspaper. In addition, placement office staffs are generally very helpful with resume and interviewing techniques.

If an employee wants to make a career change into technical support, he or she should contact the human resources department of the company or speak directly with appropriate management. In companies that are expanding their computing systems, it is often helpful for management to know that current employees would be interested in growing in a computer-related direction. They may even be willing to finance additional education.

Advancement

Technical support specialists who demonstrate leadership skills and a strong aptitude for the work may be promoted to supervisory positions within technical support departments. Supervisors are responsible for the more complicated problems that arise, as well as for some administrative duties like scheduling, interviewing, and job assignments.

Further promotion requires additional education. Some technical support specialists may become commercially certified in computer networking so that they can install, maintain, and repair computer networks. Others may prefer to pursue a bachelor's degree in computer science, either full time or part time. The range of careers available to college graduates is widely varied. Software engineers analyze industrial, business, and scientific problems and develop software programs to handle them effectively. Quality assurance engineers design automated quality assurance tests for new software applications. Systems analysts study the broad computing picture for a company or a group of companies in order to determine the best way to organize the computer systems.

There are limited opportunities for technical support specialists to be promoted into managerial positions. Doing so would require additional education in business but would probably also depend on the individual's advanced computer knowledge.

Earnings

Technical support specialist jobs are plentiful in areas where clusters of computer companies are located, such as northern California and Seattle, Washington. Median annual earnings for technical support specialists were $37,120 in 1998, according to the U.S. Department of Labor. The highest 10 percent earned more than $73,790, while the lowest 10 percent earned less than $22,930. Those with more education, responsibility, and expertise have the potential to earn much more.

Technical support specialists earned the following median annual salaries in 1997 by industry: management and public relations, $37,900; computer and office equipment, $36,300; computer and data processing services, $36,300; professional and commercial equipment, $35,700; and personnel supply services, $35,200.

Most technical support specialists work for companies that offer a full range of benefits, including health insurance, paid vacation, and sick leave. Smaller service or start-up companies may hire support specialists on a contractual basis.

Work Environment

Technical support specialists work in comfortable business environments. They generally work regular, 40-hour weeks. For certain products, however, they may be asked to work evenings or weekends or at least be on call during those times in case of emergencies. If they work for service companies, they may be required to travel to clients' sites and log overtime hours.

Technical support work can be stressful, since specialists often deal with frustrated users who may be difficult to work with. Communication problems with people less technically qualified may also be a source of frustration. Patience and understanding are essential to avoiding these problems.

Technical support specialists are expected to work quickly and efficiently and be able to perform under pressure. The ability to do this requires thorough technical expertise and keen analytical ability.

Outlook

According to the *Occupational Outlook Handbook,* 450,000 more computer support positions will be created by 2008. The U.S. Department of Labor predicts that technical support specialists will be one of the fastest growing of all occupations through the year 2008. The U.S. Department of Labor forecasts huge growth—about 100 percent—of additional support jobs through the year 2008. Every time a new computer product is released on the market or another system is installed, there will unavoidably be problems, whether from user error or technical difficulty. Therefore, there will always be a need for technical support specialists to solve the problems. Since technology changes so rapidly, it is very important for these professionals to keep up-to-date on advances. They should read trade magazines, surf the Internet, and talk with colleagues in order to know what is happening on the cutting edge.

Since some companies stop offering technical support on old products or applications after a designated time, the key is to be technically flexible. This is important for another reason as well. While the industry as a whole will require more technical support specialists in the future, it may be the case that certain computer companies go out of business. It can be a volatile industry for start-ups or young companies dedicated to the development of one product. Technical support specialists interested in working for computer companies should therefore consider living in areas in which many such companies are clustered. In this way, it will be easier to find another job if necessary.

For More Information

For information about technical support careers, contact the following organizations:

The Association for Computing Machinery

One Astor Plaza
1515 Broadway
New York, NY 10036
Tel: 212-869-7440
Email: ACMHELP@acm.org
Web: http://www.acm.org

IEEE Computer Society

1730 Massachusetts Avenue, NW
Washington, DC 20036-1992
Tel: 202-371-0101
Web: http://computer.org

Writers and Editors

Writers *are involved with expressing, editing, promoting, and interpreting ideas and facts in written form for books, magazines, trade journals, newspapers, technical studies and reports, company newsletters, radio and television broadcasts, and advertisements.*

Writers develop fiction and nonfiction ideas for plays, novels, poems, and other related works; report, analyze, and interpret facts, events, and personalities; review art, music, drama, and other artistic presentations; and persuade the general public to choose or favor certain goods, services, and personalities.

Editors *perform a wide range of functions, but their primary responsibility is to ensure that text provided by writers is suitable in content, format, and style for the intended audiences. Readers are an editor's first priority.*

The Job

Writers work in the field of communications. Specifically, they deal with the written word, whether it is destined for the printed page, broadcast, computer screen, or live theater. The nature of their work is as varied as the materials they produce: books, magazines, trade journals, newspapers, technical reports, company newsletters and other publications, advertisements, speeches, scripts for motion picture and stage productions, and scripts for radio and television broadcast. Writers develop ideas and write for all media.

Because the field of writing is so broad, workers usually specialize in a particular type of writing. For example, those who prepare scripts for motion pictures or television are called *screenwriters* or *scriptwriters*. *Playwrights* do similar writing but for theater. Those who write copy for advertisements are called *copywriters*.

Newswriters prepare stories for newspapers, radio, and television. *Columnists* specialize in writing about matters from their personal viewpoints. *Critics* review and comment upon the work of other authors, musicians, artists, and performers. In addition to all of these types of writers, there are also technical writers, novelists, biographers, poets, essayists, comedy writers, and short story writers.

Good writers gather as much information as possible about a subject and then carefully check the accuracy of their sources. Usually, this involves extensive library research and interviews or long hours of observation and personal experience. Writers keep notes from which they prepare an outline. They often rewrite sections of the material, always searching for the best way to express an idea or opinion. A manuscript may be reviewed, corrected, and revised many times before a final copy is ready.

Writers can be employed either as in-house staff or as freelancers. Pay varies according to experience and the position, but freelancers must provide their own office space and equipment such as computers and fax machines. Freelancers also are responsible for keeping tax records, sending out invoices, negotiating contracts, and providing their own health insurance.

Editors work for many kinds of publishers, publications, and corporations. Editors' titles vary widely, not only from one area of publishing to another but also within each area.

Book editors prepare written material for publication. In small publishing houses, the same editor may guide the material through all the stages of the publishing process. They may work with typesetters, printers, designers, advertising agencies, and other members of the publishing industry. In larger publishing houses, editors tend to be more specialized, being involved in only a part of the publishing process.

Acquisitions editors are the editors who find new writers and sign on new projects. They are responsible for finding new ideas for books that will sell well and for finding writers who can create the books. *Production editors* are responsible for taking the manuscript written by an author and polishing the work into a finished book. They correct grammar, spelling, and style, and check all the facts. They make sure the book reads well and suggest changes to the author if it does not. The production editor may be responsible for getting the cover designed and the art put into a book. Because the work is so demanding, production editors usually work on only one or two books at a time.

Copy editors assist the production editor in polishing the author's writing. Copy editors review each page and make all the changes required to give the book a good writing style. *Line editors* review the text to make sure specific style rules are obeyed. They make sure the same spelling is used for words where more than one spelling is correct (for example, grey and gray).

Fact checkers and *proofreaders* read the manuscript to make sure everything is spelled correctly and that all the facts in the text have been checked.

The basic functions performed by *magazine* and *newspaper editors* are much like those performed by book editors, but a significant amount of the writing that appears in magazines and newspapers, or periodicals, is done by staff writers. Periodicals often use editors who specialize in specific areas, such as *city editors,* who oversee the work of reporters who specialize in local news, and *department editors.* Department editors specialize in areas such as business, fashion, sports, and features, to name only a few. These departments are determined by the interests of the audience that the periodical intends to reach. Like book houses, periodicals use copy editors, researchers, and fact checkers, but at small periodicals, one or a few editors may be responsible for tasks that would be performed by many people at a larger publication.

Requirements

High School

High school courses that are helpful to writers and editors include English, literature, foreign languages, general science, social studies, computer science, and typing. The ability to type is almost a requisite for all positions in the communications field as is familiarity with computers.

Editors and writers must be expert communicators, so you should excel in English if you wish to work in these careers. You must learn to write extremely well, since you will be correcting and even rewriting the work of others. If elective classes in writing or editing are available in your school, take them. Study journalism and take communications courses. Work for the school paper. Take a photography class. Since virtually all editors and writers use computers, take computer courses. You absolutely must learn to type. If you cannot type accurately and rapidly, you will be at an extreme disadvantage. Don't forget, however, that a successful writer or editor must have a wide range of knowledge. The more you know about many areas, the more likely you will be to do well. Don't hesitate to explore areas that you find interesting. Do everything you can to satisfy your intellectual curiosity. As far as most writers and editors are concerned, there is no useless information.

Postsecondary Training

Competition for writing and editing jobs almost always demands the background of a college education. Many employers prefer you have a broad liberal arts background or majors in English, literature, history, philosophy, or one of the social sciences. Other employers desire communications or journalism training in college. Occasionally a master's degree in a specialized writing or editing field may be required. A number of schools offer courses in journalism and some of them offer courses or majors in book publishing, publication management, and newspaper and magazine writing.

In addition to formal course work, most employers look for practical writing and editing experience. If you have served on high school or college newspapers, yearbooks, or literary magazines, you will make a better candidate, as well as if you have worked for small community newspapers or radio stations, even in an unpaid position. Many book publishers, magazines, newspapers, and radio and television stations have summer internship programs that provide valuable training if you want to learn about the publishing and broadcasting businesses. Interns do many simple tasks, such as running errands and answering phones, but some may be asked to perform research, conduct interviews, or even write or edit some minor pieces.

Writers or editors who specialize in technical fields may need degrees, concentrated course work, or experience in specific subject areas. This applies frequently to engineering, business, or one of the sciences. Also, technical communications is a degree now offered at many universities and colleges.

If you wish to enter positions with the federal government, you will have to take a civil service examination and meet certain specified requirements, according to the type and level of position.

Other Requirements

Writers and editors should be creative and able to express ideas clearly, have a broad general knowledge, be skilled in research techniques, and be computer literate. Other assets include curiosity, persistence, initiative, resourcefulness, and an accurate memory. For some jobs—on a newspaper, for example, where the activity is hectic and deadlines short—the ability to concentrate and produce under pressure is essential.

You must be detail oriented to succeed as a writer or an editor. You must also be patient, since you may have to spend hours synthesizing information into the written word or turning a few pages of near-gibberish into powerful, elegant English. If you are the kind of person who can't sit still, you probably will not succeed in these careers. To be a good writer or editor, you must be a self-starter who is not afraid to make decisions. You must be good not only at identifying problems but also at solving them, so you must be creative.

Exploring

As a high school or college student, you can test your interest and aptitude in the fields of writing and editing by serving as a reporter or writer on school newspapers, yearbooks, and literary magazines. If you cannot work for the school paper, try to land a part-time job on a local newspaper or newsletter. If that doesn't work, you might want to publish your own newsletter. There is nothing like trying to put together a small publication to make you understand how publishing works. You may try combining another interest with your interest in writing or editing. For example, if you are interested in environmental issues, you might want to start a newsletter that deals with environmental problems and solutions in your community. Use your imagination.

Small community newspapers and local radio stations often welcome contributions from outside sources, although they may not have the resources to pay for them. Jobs in bookstores, magazine shops, and even newsstands offer a chance to become familiar with the various publications.

Information on writing and editing as a career may also be obtained by visiting local newspapers, publishers, or radio and television stations and interviewing some of the people who work there. Career conferences and other guidance programs frequently include speakers on the entire field of communications from local or national organizations.

Employers

Nearly a third of salaried writers and editors work for newspapers, magazines, and book publishers, according to the *Occupational Outlook Handbook*. Writers and editors are also employed by advertising agencies, in radio and television broadcasting, public relations firms, Internet sites, and on journals and newsletters published by business and nonprofit organizations, such as professional associations, labor unions, and religious organizations. Other employers are government agencies and film production companies.

Starting Out

A fair amount of experience is required to gain a high-level position in the writing field. Most writers start out in entry-level positions. These jobs may be listed with college placement offices, or they may be obtained by applying directly to the employment departments of the individual publishers or broadcasting companies. Graduates who previously served internships with these companies often have the advantage of knowing someone who can give them a personal recommendation. Want ads in newspapers and trade journals are another source for jobs. Because of the competition for positions, however, few vacancies are listed with public or private employment agencies.

Employers in the communications field usually are interested in samples of published writing. These are often assembled in an organized portfolio or scrapbook. Bylined or signed articles are more impressive than stories whose source is not identified.

Beginning positions as a junior writer usually involve library research, preparation of rough drafts for part or all of a report, cataloging, and other related writing tasks. These are generally carried on under the supervision of a senior writer.

Some technical writers have entered the field after working in public relations departments or as technicians or research assistants, then transferring to technical writing as openings occur. Many firms now hire writers directly upon application or recommendation of college professors and placement offices.

There is tremendous competition for editorial jobs, so it is important for a beginner who wishes to break into the business to be as well prepared as possible. College students who have gained experience as interns, have worked for publications during the summers, or have attended special programs in publishing will be at an advantage. In addition, applicants for any editorial position must be extremely careful when preparing cover letters and resumes. Even a single error in spelling or usage will disqualify an applicant. Applicants for editorial or proofreading positions must also expect to take and pass tests that are designed to determine their language skills.

Many editors enter the field as editorial assistants or proofreaders. Some editorial assistants perform only clerical tasks, whereas others may also proofread or perform basic editorial tasks. Typically, an editorial assistant who performs well will be given the opportunity to take on more and more editorial duties as time passes. Proofreaders have the advantage of being able to look at the work of editors, so they can learn while they do their own work.

Good sources of information about job openings are school placement offices, classified ads in newspapers and trade journals, specialized publications such as *Publishers Weekly* (a good source of jobs in book publishing), and Internet sites. One way to proceed is to identify local publishers through the Yellow Pages. Many publishers have Web sites that list job openings, and large publishers often have telephone job lines that serve the same purpose.

Advancement

Most writers find their first jobs as editorial or production assistants. Advancement may be more rapid in small companies, where beginners learn by doing a little bit of everything and may be given writing tasks immediately. In large firms, duties are usually more compartmentalized. Assistants in entry-level positions are assigned such tasks as research, fact checking, and copyrighting, but it generally takes much longer to advance to full-scale writing duties.

Promotion into more responsible positions may come with the assignment of more important articles and stories to write, or it may be the result of moving to another company. Freelance or self-employed writers earn advancement in the form of larger fees as they gain exposure and establish their reputations.

In book houses, employees who start as editorial assistants or proofreaders and show promise generally become copy editors. After gaining skill in that position, they may be given a wider range of duties while retaining the same title. The next step may be a position as a *senior copy editor,* which involves overseeing the work of junior copy editors, or as a *project editor.* The project editor performs a wide variety of tasks, including copyediting, coordinating the work of in-house and freelance copy editors, and managing the schedule of a particular project. From this position, an editor may move up to become first assistant editor, then *managing editor,* then *editor-in-chief.* These positions involve more management and decision making than is usually found in the positions described previously. The editor-in-chief works with the publisher to ensure that a suitable editorial policy is being followed, while the managing editor is responsible for all aspects of the editorial department. The *assistant editor* provides support to the managing editor.

Newspaper editors generally begin working on the copy desk, where they progress from less significant stories and projects to major news and feature stories. A common route to advancement is for copy editors to be promoted to a particular department, where they may move up the ranks to management positions. An editor who has achieved success in a department may become a city editor, who is responsible for news, or a managing editor, who runs the entire editorial operation of a newspaper.

Magazine editors advance in much the same way that book editors do. After they become copy editors, they work their way up to become senior editors, managing editors, and editors-in-chief. In many cases, magazine editors advance by moving from a position on one magazine to the same position with a larger or more prestigious magazine. Such moves often bring significant increases in both pay and status.

Earnings

In 1998, median annual earnings for writers and editors were $36,480 a year, according to the *Occupational Outlook Handbook.* The lowest 10 percent earned less than $20,920, while the highest 10 percent earned $76,660. Earnings of those in administrative and supervisory positions are somewhat higher. Experienced writers and researchers are paid $40,000 and over, depending on their qualifications and the size of the publication they work on. In book publishing, some divisions pay better than others.

In addition to their salaries, many writers and editors earn some income from freelance work. Part-time freelancers may earn from $5,000 to $15,000 a year. Freelance earnings vary widely. Full-time established freelance writers and editors may earn up to $75,000 a year.

Work Environment

Working conditions vary for writers. Although the workweek usually runs 35 to 40 hours, many writers work overtime. A publication that is issued frequently has more deadlines closer together, creating greater pressures to meet them. The work is especially hectic on newspapers and at broadcasting companies, which operate seven days a week. Writers often work nights and weekends to meet deadlines or to cover a late-developing story.

Most writers work independently, but they often must cooperate with artists, photographers, rewriters, and advertising people who may have widely differing ideas of how the materials should be prepared and presented.

Physical surroundings range from comfortable private offices to noisy, crowded newsrooms filled with other workers typing and talking on the telephone. Some writers must confine their research to the library or telephone interviews, but others may travel to other cities or countries or to local sites, such as theaters, ballparks, airports, factories, or other offices.

The work is arduous, but writers are seldom bored. Each day brings new and interesting problems. The jobs occasionally require travel. The most difficult element is the continual pressure of deadlines. People who are the most content as writers enjoy and work well with deadline pressure.

The environments in which editors work vary widely. For the most part, publishers of all kinds realize that a quiet atmosphere is conducive to work that requires tremendous concentration. It takes an unusual ability to focus to edit in a noisy place. Most editors work in private offices or cubicles. Book editors often work in quieter surroundings than do newspaper editors or quality-control people in advertising agencies, who sometimes work in rather loud and hectic situations.

Even in relatively quiet surroundings, however, editors often have many distractions. A project editor who is trying to do some copyediting or review the editing of others may, for example, have to deal with phone calls from authors, questions from junior editors, meetings with members of the editorial and production staff, and questions from freelancers, among many other distractions. In many cases, editors have computers that are exclusively for their own use, but in others, editors must share computers that are located in a common area.

Deadlines are an important issue for virtually all editors. Newspaper and magazine editors work in a much more pressurized atmosphere than book editors because they face daily or weekly deadlines, whereas book production usually takes place over several months.

In almost all cases, editors must work long hours during certain phases of the editing process. Some newspaper editors start work at 5 AM, others work until 11 PM or even through the night. Feature editors, columnists, and editorial page editors usually can schedule their day in a more regular fashion, as can editors who work on weekly newspapers. Editors working on hard news, however, may receive an assignment that must be completed, even if work extends well into the next shift.

Outlook

The employment of writers and editors is expected to increase faster than the average rate of all occupations through 2008, according to the *Occupational Outlook Handbook*. The demand for writers and editors by newspapers, periodicals, book publishers, and nonprofit organizations is expected to increase. There will be increasing job opportunities for writers and editors in Internet publishing as online publishing and services continue to grow. Advertising and public relations will also provide job opportunities.

The major book and magazine publishers, broadcasting companies, advertising agencies, public relations firms, and the federal government account for the concentration of writers and editors in large cities such as New York, Chicago, Los Angeles, Boston, Philadelphia, San Francisco, and Washington, DC. Opportunities in small newspapers, corporations, and professional, religious, business, technical, and trade publications can be found throughout the country.

People entering this field should realize that the competition for jobs is extremely keen. Beginners, especially, may have difficulty finding employment. Of the thousands who graduate each year with degrees in English, journalism, communications, and the liberal arts, intending to establish a career as writer or editor, many turn to other occupations when they find that applicants far outnumber the job openings available. College students would do well to keep this in mind and prepare for an unrelated alternate career in the event they are unable to obtain a position as writer; another benefit of this approach is that, at the same time, they will become qualified as writers or editors in a specialized field. The practicality of preparing for alternate careers is borne out by the fact that opportunities are best in firms that prepare business and trade publications and in technical writing and editing.

For More Information

The following organization is an excellent source of information about careers in copyediting. The ACES organizes educational seminars and maintains lists of internships.
American Copy Editors Society (ACES)
> 3 Healy Street
> Huntington, NY 11743
> Tel: 800-393-7681
> Web: http://www.copydesk.org

The AAP is an organization of book publishers. Its extensive Web site is a good place to begin learning about the book business.
Association of American Publishers (AAP)
> 71 Fifth Avenue
> New York, NY 10010-2368
> Tel: 212-255-0200
> Email: aphillips@publishers.org
> Web: http://www.publishers.org

The Fund provides information about internships and about the newspaper business in general.
Dow Jones Newspaper Fund
PO Box 300
Princeton, NJ 08543-0300
Tel: 609-452-2820
Email: newsfund@wsj.dowjones.com
Web: http://www.dowjones.com/newsfund/

The EFA is an organization for freelance editors. Members receive a newsletter and a free listing in their directory.
Editorial Freelancers Association (EFA)
71 West 23rd Street, Suite 1504
New York, NY 10010
Tel: 212-929-5400
Web: http://www.the-efa.org

The MPA is a good source of information about internships.
Magazine Publishers of America (MPA)
919 Third Avenue, 22nd Floor
New York, NY 10022
Tel: 212-872-3700
Web: http://www.magazine.org

Information on writing and editing careers in the field of communications is available from:
National Association of Science Writers
PO Box 294
Greenlawn, NY 11740
Tel: 631-757-5664
Web: http://www.nasw.org/

This organization offers student memberships for those interested in opinion writing.
National Conference of Editorial Writers
6223 Executive Boulevard
Rockville, MD 20852
Tel: 301-984-3015
Email: ncewhqs@erols.com
Web: http://www.ncew.org

Index

A

Account executives, 63
Acquisitions editors, 181
Advanced practice nurses, 128
Advertising account executives, **3–7**
American Academy of Family
  Physicians, 116
American Advertising Federation, 7
American Association for Paralegal
  Education, 105
American Association of Advertising
  Agencies, 7
American Association of Colleges of
  Nursing, 133
American Association of University
  Professors, 12–13, 14
American Bar Association, 105
American Center for Design, 74
American College of Health Care
  Administrators, 85
American College of Healthcare
  Executives, 85
American Copy Editors Society, 189
American Federation of Teachers, 14,
  140
American Institute of Certified Public
  Accountants, 99
American Institute of Graphic Arts, 74
American Management Association,
  99
American Marketing Association, 7
American Medical Association, 116
American Medical College Application
  Service, 109
American Nurses' Association, 133

American Police Academy, 124
Applications programmers, 32, 151
Assistant editor, 186
Assistant professor, 8, 12, 13
Associate professor, 8, 12–13
Association for Computing Machinery,
  31, 38, 79, 156, 164, 179
Association for Systems Management,
  46
Association of American Medical
  Colleges, 109, 116
Association of American Publishers,
  189
Association of Information Technology
  Professionals, 38, 46, 52
Association of Internal Management
  Consultants, 98
Association of Legal Administrators,
  106
Association of Management Consulting
  Firms, 99
Association of Medical Illustrators, 89,
  90, 91
Association of University Programs in
  Health Administration, 85

B

Book editors, 181

C

Calligraphers, 86
Canadian Association of Schools of
  Social Work, 149
Center for Futures Education, 21

Certified Network Professional program, 27
Chicago Board of Trade, 20, 22
Chicago Board Options Exchange, 22
Chicago Mercantile Exchange, 22
Chief business programmers, 32
Chief engineer, 59
Chief of nuclear medicine, 108
Child care/family services workers, 142–143
Chronicle of Higher Education, 12
City editors, 182
Coffee, Sugar & Cocoa Exchange, Inc., 23
College professors, **8–14**
Columnists, 181
Committee on Allied Health Education and Accreditation of the American Medical Association, 88, 89
Commodities brokers, **15–23**
Commodity Education Institute, 17
Community health nurses, 127, 131
Computer graphic designers, 72
Computer hardware engineers, 75
Computer network administrators, **24–31**
Computer programmers, **32–38,** 150
Computer systems/programmer analysts, **39–46**
Copy editors, 181–182
Copywriters, 180
Corporate paralegal, 100
Council of Administrators of Special Education, 170
Council on Social Work Education, 144, 149
Court administrator paralegal, 100–101
Critics, 181

D
Database administrators, 47, 48
Database managers, 47, 48, 49
Database specialists, **47–52**
Delphian School, 57, 62
Department editors, 182
Discount brokers, 16
Dow Jones Newspaper Fund, 190

E
Editorial assistants, 185
Editorial Freelancers Association, 190
Editor-in-chief, 186
Editors, **180–190**
Electrical engineers, **53–62**
Electronic Industries Alliance, 62
Electronics engineers, **53–62**
Engagement manager, 97

F
Fact checkers, 182
Family practitioners, 107
Fashion illustrators, 86, 87, 88, 89, 90, 91
Field service engineers, 55
Financial services brokers, **63–67**
Flight surgeon, 108
Floor brokers, 16, 17
Floor manager, 19
Full professor, 8, 12
Full service brokers, 15–16
Future commission merchants, 15

G
General duty nurses, 126
General practitioners, 107
Gerontological social workers, 143
Graphic Artists Guild, 92

Graphic designers, **68–74**

Guild of Natural Science Illustrators, 92

H

Hardware engineers, **75–79**

Head nurses, 126

Health care managers, **80–85**

Health/mental health care social workers, 142

Health services administrators, 64, 80

Health services managers, 80

Help desk specialists, 173

Highway patrol officers, 118

I

IEEE Computer Society, 29, 31, 79, 154, 156, 164, 179

Illustrators, **86–92**

Industrial nurses, 127, 131

Industrial physicians, 107–108

Information system programmers, 33

Information systems managers, 47

Institute for Certification of Computing Professionals, 34, 38, 41–42, 46, 50, 52, 76, 79, 163

Institute of Electrical and Electronics Engineers, 61, 79

Institute of Management Consultants, 95, 99

Instructor, 12

Internal affairs investigators, 118

International Academy of Merchandising and Design, 92

Introducing brokers, 16

J

Junior Engineering Technical Society, 57, 627

Junior partners, 97

L

Legal assistants, 100

Line editors, 182

M

Magazine editors, 182, 187, 188

Magazine Publishers of America, 190

Management analysts and consultants, **93–99**

Managing editor, 186

Maturity nurses, 126

Medical College Admission Test, 109

Medical illustrators, 86–87, 88, 89, 90, 91

Medical officers, 107

Michigan Technological University Summer Youth Program, 62

Microcomputer support specialists, 174

MidAmerica Commodity Exchange, 23

Minneapolis Grain Exchange, 23

N

National Academy of Sciences Institute of Medicine, 115

National Association for Practical Nurse Education and Service, Inc., 133

National Association of Legal Assistants Certifying Board, 101–102, 105

National Association of Schools of Art and Design, 70, 74

National Association of Science Writers, 190

National Association of Securities Dealers, 21, 64–65, 67

National Association of Social Workers, 142, 149

National Clearinghouse for Professions in Special Education, Council for Exceptional Children, 171
National Commodities Futures Examination, 17
National Conference of Editorial Writers, 190
National Council for Accreditation of Teacher Education, 140
National Education Association, 140
National Federation of Paralegal Associations, 101–102, 106
National Futures Association, 17, 22
National Health Council, 85
National League for Nursing, 133
National Paralegal Association, 106
National Police Officers Association of America, 125
National United Law Enforcement Officers Association, 125
Network control operators, 25–26
Network engineers, 29–30
Network managers, 29
Network Professional Association, 27, 29, 31
Network security specialists, 25
Network specialists, 24, 30
Network systems administrators, 26
Newspaper editors, 182, 186–187, 188
Newswriters, 181
New York Futures Exchange, 23
New York Mercantile Exchange, 23
Numerical control tool programmers, 33–34
Nursing service director, 126–127

O
Occupational health nurses, 127
Occupational physicians, 107–108

Office nurses, 127, 131

P
Paralegals, **100–106**
Pew Health Professions Commission, 115
Philadelphia Board of Trade, 22
Physicians, **107–116**
Playwrights, 180
Police officer commanding officers III, 118
Police officers, **117–125**
Police officers III, 118
Principals, 97
Private duty nurses, 127
Process control programmers, 33
Production editors, 181
Production engineers, 55
Professors, 55
Programmer-analyst, 32
Project editor, 186, 188
Project team leaders, 161–162
Proofreaders, 182, 185
Public health nurses, 127

R
Registered nurses, **126–133**
Registered representatives, 63
Runner, 18

S
Sales engineer, 55
School nurses, 127
School social workers, 143
Screenwriters, 180
Scriptwriters, 180
Secondary school teachers, **134–140**
Securities Industry Association, 67
Securities sales representatives, 63

Securities trades, 63–64
Senior copy editor, 186
Senior engagement mangers, 97
Social workers, **141–149**
Society for Environmental Graphic
    Design, 74
Society of Illustrators, 91
Society of Publication Designers, 73, 74
Software and Information Industry
    Association, 163
Software designers, **150–156**
Software engineering technicians, 158
Software engineers, **157–164**
Special education teachers, **165–171**
State police officers, 117, 118
State troopers, 118
Stockbrokers, 63

Supervisors (nursing), 126
Surgical nurses, 126
Systems analyst, 39
Systems programmers, 32, 39

T
Technical support specialists, **172–179**
Technical writers, 185
Trader, 15

U
User support specialists, 173

W
Webmaster, 26
Writers, **180–190**